ACCELERATED LEARNING HANDBOOK

Master New Skills Effortlessly and Faster

by Speeding Up Your Learning Process

Damien Weston

ISBN: 978-1915218070

First Edition: October 2021

All rights reserved © 2021 by Damien Weston

This book is copyright protected, and it is only for personal use. You cannot amend, distribute, sell, use, quote, or paraphrase any part of this book's content without the author or publisher's consent. All pictures contained in this book come from the author's archive or copyright-free stock websites (Canva, Pixabay, Pexel, Freepix, Unsplash, StockSnap, etc.).

Disclaimer Notice:

Please note the information contained within this document is for educational and entertainment purposes only. All effort has been executed to present accurate, up-to-date, reliable, complete information. No warranties of any kind are declared or implied. Readers acknowledge that the author is not engaged in rendering legal, financial, medical or professional advice. The content within this book has been derived from various sources. Please consult a licensed professional before attempting any techniques outlined in this book.

By reading this document, the reader agrees that under no circumstances is the author responsible for any losses, direct or indirect, that are incurred due to the use of the information contained within this document, including, but not limited to, errors, omissions, or inaccuracies.

The trademarks used are without any consent, and the publication of the trademark is without permission or backing by the trademark owner. All trademarks and brands within this book are for clarifying purposes only and are owned by the owners themselves, not affiliated with this document.

TABLE OF CONTENTS

- INTRODUCTION 1
- THE LEARNING PROCESS 5
  - Create a roadmap to learn effectively 8
  - The psychology of learning 14
  - Different learning styles 17
- ABOUT OUR MEMORY 23
  - What is memory? 23
  - The three types of memory 25
  - How is memory processed? 31
  - Why do we fail to remember? 33
  - How to improve memory 35
- ACCELERATED LEARNING 41
  - Why do we fail at learning? 43
  - Two primary resources for learning 45
  - About accelerated learning 46
  - Better learning 48
  - The principles of accelerated learning 50
- SPEED READING 53
  - What is speed reading? 53
  - Benefits of speed reading 56
  - The fastest speed readers in the world 61
- START YOUR TRAINING 67
  - Goal setting 68

Getting ready 69

Understand your current level 72

Basic reading issues 75

SPEED READING TECHNIQUES 81

The 9-step method for reading faster 82

Practical tips to increase your reading speed 95

How to measure your reading speed 102

TRAINING EXERCISES 105

Simple speed reading test 106

Example of speed reading drill 108

Reading comprehension exercises – Skimming and scanning 110

Eye exercises for speed reading 115

HOW TO READ FASTER AND RETAIN MORE 119

Hacks for accelerating your reading 120

How to improve reading retention 125

SPEED LISTENING 129

Increase your content consumption 129

The content's quality becomes less important 130

Reduce the time cost 131

Drawbacks 132

Getting started 133

CONCLUSION 135

INTRODUCTION

The mind processes these objects so quickly that you aren't even aware of them. Simply moving the eyes in a specific direction causes them to sense and recognize what is there.

Things aren't quite as smooth and fluid when we listen, though. Processing words and the meaning expressed by those words requires time and effort. Reading is a demanding task that requires a lot of mental energy for many people, and some people find it so taxing that they don't read at all.

So, why can't the text be processed in the same way as other items in our world are?

We can do it!

In fact, since the eyes are closely attached to the brain, many people mistake them for extensions of the brain rather than distinct organs. According to scientists, visual information processing takes up to 65 percent of the brain.

If the eyes are the body's second most complex organ, the brain is the most complex. Many believe it to be the most complex structure in the world, surpassing planets, stars, and even airplanes. Every thinking, behavior, memory, feeling, and experience we have in the world is driven by the brain.

Within minutes of reading any of the pages, you can double or even triple your current reading speed, and you can speed up even further after practicing the additional suggestions. There's no doubt that if you put in the effort, you'll be able to read a 200-page book in an hour!

Reading and comprehension go hand in hand, so you'll learn to develop your comprehension as well as your reading speed. After all, the aim of reading more quickly is to gain more knowledge. What good is speed reading if we can't understand and remember what we're reading? It's not speed-reading if you don't improve your comprehension.

Today, we all have to cope with more information than ever before, and if you can't keep up, you'll soon fall behind.

The basic truth is that there is so much information available to us in more forms and formats than ever before, being pushed to us on a daily basis in more ways than ever before, that traditional techniques of dealing with information are no longer effective. They're just too slow. You will fail if you try to learn what you need or want to know today at a regular, traditional, "pre-digital age" learning speed.

That's where this book comes in.

I've always had a voracious thirst for learning, information, and productivity hacks, but it wasn't until I became a single parent with a toddler that I realized I had both an urgent need for new information (ask any new parent!) and was hopelessly time-poor. Out of sheer desperation to learn more, quicker, I became laser-focused and tracked out, developed, and improved the approaches disclosed in this course.

These strategies have saved (and gained) me a tremendous amount of time, allowing me to get through hundreds of hours of content in multiple formats in a fraction of the time.

You can now do the same.

Students, professionals, and anyone else who finds themselves with more things to learn, will find the solution to their problem inside this book.

Anyone can implement the instructions in this guide. What you need is just the will to succeed, everything else you will find in the next pages. Happy reading!

THE LEARNING PROCESS

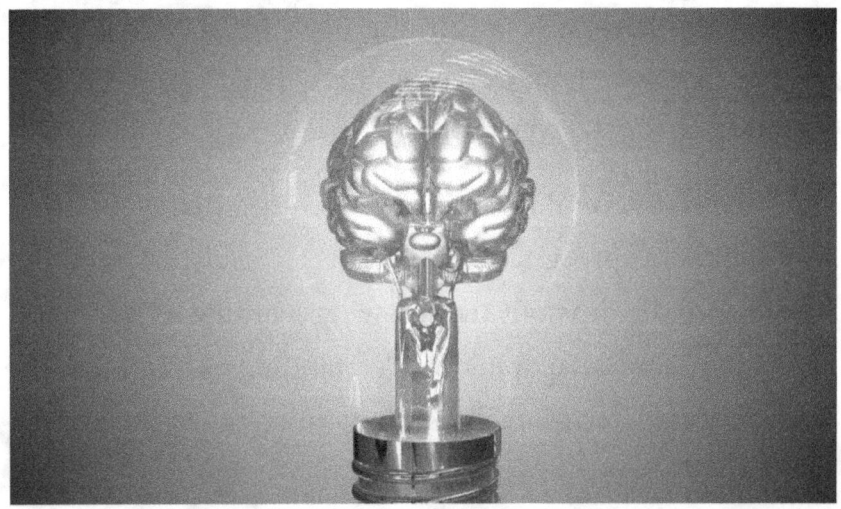

Learning is as necessary as breathing to being human. It is something we all do, consciously and unconsciously, throughout our lives, at work, school, and at home. But what actually is learning? What exactly does it mean to learn?

For a long of human history, people assumed that the ability to learn was synonymous with intelligence. "If you're intelligent, you can learn." Today's research supports a quite different result.

Yet, far too little has changed in terms of how people learn. As a society, we require richer kinds of education in which information and knowledge coexist with the creativity and problem-solving skills required in today's market.

For a long time, experts argued that education was all about facts, dates, and details. The objective was to learn in order to become knowledgeable. If you were able to apply your information, it signified you had learnt something. It turns out that this approach to learning does not always work in today's society. It also contradicts what research has demonstrated to be effective.

Over the last several decades, research has discovered that learning is a process rather than a result of inherent intelligence. It turns out that viewing learning as a method or system for developing understanding is significantly more accurate. Learning does not happen on its own based on your IQ or general aptitude.

Many other skills are required for learning, such as focusing and directing your attention, planning and sticking to a program, perseverance, resilience, and the ability to reflect on information. The difference between mastery and rote review is using a method to learn – or, more accurately, learning how to learn. This is the only way to attain truly effective learning.

It has been demonstrated that the precise procedure or method of learning adopted reliably predicts achievement. Experts discovered a stunning, consistent discovery after examining decades of study. Learning approaches have a significant impact on outcomes in a variety of professional domains. Scientists were able to accurately estimate students' GPAs based on the learning technique they used.

However, learning as a process is about more than research, results, and prediction. Memorizing facts has become less valuable due to the internet's pervasiveness and our fluctuating attention spans. Details, logistics, and facts are often handled for us by technology. Instead, the bigger concerns are: how do our brains truly operate, and how do we master them?

Finding the greatest way to study in the first place necessitates setting strict goals. What exactly do you want or need to learn?

Struggles and setbacks should be expected within the confines of these goals. Even still, most people require the assurance that their efforts will be rewarded in the end. Goals should be realistic enough to make learning feel possible and ambitious enough to pique your interest.

Ambition for a goal can sometimes carry us through adversity and hardship on the way. Recognizing that hardship is often a necessary aspect of learning keeps us from becoming too frustrated and giving up completely. To put it another way, 'learning is a process.'

Learning as a process implies that we may improve our ability to obtain expertise by method, effort, focus, and practice.

Create a roadmap to learn effectively

Here are six stages to highlight the key areas required for effective learning.

Finding value

Learning dies without motivation. To engage the fray of difficulty and misery that is learning, the topic must be significant or valuable. Finding significance is why we decide to devote our efforts and stick to our goals in the face of failures. In summary, we need some type of motivation to study. Learning is about instilling purpose in one's life. The ability to connect one topic to another can make learning considerably easier. Consider a favorite activity or topic and consider how it can be related to the new field of interest. Involve someone you know or care about. Sew something for someone you care about if you want to learn to sew.

The other essential tool is to make learning active and meaningful. We mean cognitively active when we say "active." So, as you learn or study something, ask yourself a lot of questions. What exactly does this mean? What difference does it make? Could you please explain to a friend?

Setting targets

Focus is essential for learning, and the utilization of specific targets raises your chances of mastery significantly.

According to research, those who have a defined plan and goals outperform others. People who want to study must first decide what they want to master.

Learning is also known as knowledge management. Success, as in professional management, needs planning, goals, and timetables. Setting goals entails developing clear targets that are free of ambiguity or generalization. Realistic, explicit objectives keep students from becoming disheartened.

It can be difficult to visualize reaching a goal that is too broad or abstract. Because the goal is too far in the future, the learner may lose motivation. On the other hand, rigor in selecting your learning objectives is critical. Learning material should be hard rather than easy or based on previously learned principles.

Experiment with concepts that are a little outside your comfort zone, and this is where learning takes place.

At the same time, make an effort to study in bite-sized portions. To learn knowledge, we must have a determined method for acquiring that knowledge and organizing it logically. Set aside time for learning and try to study for 30 minutes in increments of 30 minutes.

Also, consider structuring your learning in ways that build on earlier information. What you know is, indeed, the best predictor of what you can learn.

Braindumps are especially effective. Simply put, after studying something, we should jot down our thoughts. No matter what you call it, use this quick retrieval method throughout your instruction before the school year's conclusion. This is how it works: Put a stop to your class, lecture, or activity. Instruct students to jot down anything they can recall. 'Continue with your lesson, lecture, or activity.'

Developing knowledge

At some point, actions should be taken to strengthen current knowledge and pursue challenges that go beyond what has already been done. Time must be set aside to practice and further build the foundations of knowledge gathered thus far.

However, not all practice is created equal. Superior practice necessitates being intellectually alert with the mind at work. Rote memorization and re-reading, for example, are not active techniques of practice or learning. Non-passive strategies, such as making little examinations and quizzes or visualizing discussing the topic to a third party, are far superior.

Learning should not only build on previous work, but it should also have the ability to resurrect past, related themes. According to well-known research, pupils who tried to recall a section without looking at it remembered it more deeply than those who just read it over and again. For example, after reading this article, designing a quiz of similar questions would provide more learning benefits than going over the material again.

To put it simply, there is no such thing as effortless learning, and all learning requires effort.

Extending expertise

It's vital to put your knowledge to use once you've developed a solid foundation of information. Accumulated knowledge or experience can be increased when applied to real-world situations. If you want to learn a language, go to the place where it is spoken. Try practicing the ability you'd like to improve.

If you want to improve your Powerpoint presentation skills, you should present more frequently. You can also broaden your knowledge via self-questioning and self-explanation. "Is this genuinely logical?" you should ask yourself. Why is it one way and not another? One of the most effective ways to learn is to make an idea clear to another person or to yourself. Working as part of a team offers this advantage: by exchanging information, each team member has the potential to improve.

Teaching as a learning strategy is undeniably tough. It is vital to maintain our affective or emotional selves when learning new things. Maintain morale by keeping track of improvements and development.

Relating skills

Topics gradually link through learning. If we develop value by looking at the big picture, any minor detail or point is less intriguing than the overall. The whole is about how the picture interacts, and various themes are related. What are the main concepts that make a topic make sense?

Thought experiments or hypotheticals might help you understand the bigger picture. Albert Einstein frequently used these. This can be applied to many domains, but in biology, it is conceivable to envisage a counterfactual in which evolution never occurs. Take the climax or peak story point in a great piece of literature and envision the inverse.

To see relationships emerge in a mass of knowledge, graphic organizers, brain or concept mapping can all be used. Visually viewing how different bits of information or skills link on a page helps to increase knowledge. By combining themes, you can see the same information in various ways, and combining makes connections more evident.

This section is about seeing beyond the obvious. What's the larger picture in terms of how this topic relates to others? Pose questions regarding the relationships between topics. How does this topic work? Consider the situation in a broad sense.

Ultimately, this means beginning by thinking like a subject matter expert. Plant biology can be learned by thinking like a plant biologist and understanding neuroscience by thinking about it as a genuine neuroscientist.

Rethinking understanding

Making mistakes is a common part of learning, and in reality, it is unavoidable. Arrogance is one of the most common errors that can be made: believing that we know everything there is to know. Instead, to gain true knowledge, we must examine what we already know. Rethink what you believe you know for sure.

Turning to other sources or others increases the likelihood of gaining a fresh perspective. When presented with conflicting systems of thought, your learning style improves. Teams that are made up of people from various backgrounds perform better.

When you're stuck on a topic or question, try addressing it to someone in a different field or with a different life experience than you. In order to find innovative solutions in a corporation, for example, ask the cleaning staff for suggestions.

Finally, assess what knowledge or abilities have been acquired near the end of a learning process. Have any of your previous thought processes changed? What is the relationship between this content and the rest of your knowledge bases? In a nutshell, have I learned anything? What comes next?

The psychology of learning

Psychologists frequently define learning as a generally permanent change in behavior as a result of experience. The psychology of learning is concerned with various issues concerning how people learn and interact with their surroundings.

John B. Watson, a psychologist, was one of the first to investigate how learning affects behavior, proposing that all behaviors are the outcome of the learning process. Watson's findings gave rise to a school of thinking known as behaviorism. The behavioral school of thinking recommended investigating interior thoughts, memories, and other subjective mental processes.

The behaviorists argued that psychology should be the scientific study of observable behavior. During the first half of the twentieth century, behaviorism flourished and made significant contributions to our knowledge of some essential learning processes.

Are you ready for a huge test in your learning psychology class? Or are you simply looking for a review of learning and behavioral psychology topics? This learning study guide provides an overview of some major learning concerns, such as behaviorism, classical conditioning, and operant conditioning.

Let's learn a little more about learning psychology.

Learning

Learning can be described in various ways, but most psychologists would agree that it is a generally permanent change in behavior that occurs as a result of experience. During the first part of the twentieth century, a school of thought known as behaviorism grew to dominate psychology, seeking to explain the learning process.

Classical conditioning, operant conditioning, and observational learning are the three major types of learning defined by behavioral psychology.

Behaviorism

Behaviorism was a psychological school of thought that tried to measure solely observable behaviors.

John B. Watson founded it and articulated it in his seminal 1913 work Psychology as the Behaviorist Views. It argued that psychology was an experimental and objective science and that interior mental processes should not be examined because they could not be immediately viewed and measured.

Watson's work included the well-known Little Albert experiment, in which he trained a young kid to fear a white rat. For much of the early twentieth century, behaviorism dominated psychology. While behavioral techniques remain significant today, the later half of the twentieth century saw the rise of humanistic psychology, biological psychology, and cognitive psychology.

Classical conditioning

Classical conditioning is a learning process in which a previously neutral stimulus is associated with a stimulus that naturally elicits a response.

In Pavlov's classic experiment, for example, the naturally occurring stimulus that was coupled with the previously neutral ringing of the bell was the smell of food. Once a link was established between the two, the sound of the bell may elicit a reaction.

Operant conditioning

Operant conditioning is a learning process that increases or decreases the likelihood of a response occurring as a result of reinforcement or punishment. The core theory of operant conditioning, which was first researched by Edward Thorndike and then by B.F. Skinner, is that the consequences of our actions impact voluntary conduct.

Skinner described how reinforcement might lead to increases in behaviors while punishment can lead to declines. He also discovered that the timing of reinforcements determined how quickly a behavior was learned and how strong the response was. Schedules of reinforcement describe the timing and rate of reinforcement.

Observational learning

Observational learning is the process of learning by observing and copying others. According to Albert Bandura's social learning theory, in addition to conditioning, humans learn through seeing and imitating the actions of others.

People will copy the actions of others without direct reward, as illustrated by his famed "Bobo Doll" tests. Attention, motor skills, motivation, and memory are four critical components for efficient observational learning.

Different learning styles

Many individuals acknowledge that everyone has distinct learning styles and strategies that they like. Learning styles are the most frequent methods in which people learn. Everyone possesses a variety of learning methods. Some people may discover that they have a dominant learning style, with significantly less use of the other forms. Others may discover that they employ different styles in different situations. There is no such thing as a perfect combination, and your fashion sense isn't either. You can improve your ability in less prevalent styles as well as styles that you already know how to employ successfully.

Learning with diverse learning styles and "many intelligences" is a relatively new technique. Educators have just recently begun to recognize this method. Traditional education relied on (and continues to rely on) linguistic and logical teaching approaches. It also employs a limited set of learning and teaching methods. Many schools continue to rely on classroom and book-based instruction, extensive repetition and timed tests for reinforcement and revision. As a result, persons who employ these learning styles and strategies are sometimes labeled "bright." Those that employ less preferred learning styles frequently find themselves in lesser classrooms, with various unflattering names and, in some cases, lower-quality teaching. This can lead to both positive and negative spirals, reinforcing the notion that one is "clever" or "stupid."

You can apply approaches that are more suited to you if you recognize and understand your individual learning patterns. This speeds up and increases the quality of your learning.

The seven different learning styles

- Visual (spatial): Visual or spatial learners are said to retain information better when they see pictures or images and respond well to colors and mind maps.
- Aural (auditory-musical): After hearing information, aural or auditory-musical learners should retain the

majority of it. Listen to your favorite song: Do you tune out or recall more than if you read the transcript?

- Verbal (linguistic): Verbal, or linguistic, learners are expected to respond well to written or spoken words by employing tools such as rhymes and acronyms.
- Physical (kinesthetic): Kinaesthetic learners, as per theory, are all about doing things physically. Role-playing, using flashcards, or physically performing the task can all help kids learn more effectively.
- Logical (mathematical): In order to learn effectively, logical or mathematical learners employ logic and structures. If you're good with figures and statistics, you might benefit from the logical style.
- Social (interpersonal): Social or interpersonal, learners are designed to perform best when they engage in study activities with others, such as quizzing one other or participating in a study group.
- Solitary (intrapersonal): Solitary, or intrapersonal, learners are said to work best by themselves. When studying on your own, taking notes and reciting them back to yourself might be beneficial. Most of us will need to conduct some solo revision at some point in our life.

Why are learning styles important?

Recognize the fundamentals of learning styles

Your learning styles have a greater impact than you may believe. Your preferred learning styles direct how you learn, and they also alter how you internally represent experiences, recall information, and even the language you use. This chapter delves deeper into these aspects.

According to research, each learning style engages various areas of the brain. We recall more of what we learn when we engage more of the brain during learning. Using brain-imaging technologies, researchers were able to identify the critical areas of the brain involved for each learning type.

As an example:

- The visual sense is managed by the occipital lobes in the back of the brain. The occipital and parietal lobes both control spatial orientation.
- Aural material is handled by the temporal lobes. For music, the right temporal lobe is very crucial.
- Verbal: The temporal and frontal lobes, particularly two specialized areas known as the Broca's and Wernicke's areas (in the left hemisphere of these two lobes).
- Physical movement is controlled by the cerebellum and the motor cortex (located at the back of the frontal lobe).
- Logical thought is driven by the parietal lobes, particularly the left side.

- Social: Much of our social activities are handled by the frontal and temporal lobes. The limbic system (seen separately from the hippocampus) influences both social and solitary behavior. The limbic system is heavily involved in emotions, moods, and aggression.
- Solitary: This style activates the frontal and parietal lobes, as well as the emotional system.

ABOUT OUR MEMORY

When you think of memory, you usually think of that amazing time in your life. Perhaps you recall a good childhood experience or a person you used to know who was important to you. However, memory is much more than that. Reading, walking, and recognizing the aroma of your favorite cuisine are all made possible through memory. But what does this have to do with human memory? How does it function?

What is memory?

Our ability to encode, retain, and remember information from our brain is referred to as memory. But what exactly does this mean? We will go through this process in the following order:

Encoding

All of the information that our brain gets through our senses must first be converted into a form that the memory can store. Perception through the senses is the first step in this event. *How* the information is encoded is determined by the type of information and the senses through which *your brain acquires it*. Furthermore, mood can influence what is encoded and stored in the memory. A stressful scenario, for example, can cause your brain to prevent you from retaining memories at all.

Storing

After all of the received information has been encoded, the brain can store it in memory. However, there is no unique location within the human brain where all memories are kept. The many types of memories are stored in several corresponding regions of the brain.

Retrieving

This stage refers to the process of re-accessing information stored in the memory. When you recall a good childhood memory, for example, you are accessing information that was stored in your memory years ago. Although it may appear that you recall a single memory, recalling a smell, sight, sound, or feeling are all individual memories stored in different regions of the brain. When recalling a memory, you contact various sections of your brain and connect those bits of information.

How long do memories last?

Some memories are quite transient, lasting only a few seconds, and allow us to absorb sensory information about our surroundings.

Short-term memories are slightly longer and last between 20 and 30 seconds. These memories are primarily made up of what we are currently focusing on and thinking about.

Finally, some memories are capable of persisting for days, weeks, months, or even decades. The majority of these long-term memories exist outside of our immediate awareness, but they can be brought into consciousness as needed.

The three types of memory

As previously stated, human memory does not exist as a single sort of memory, and it is made up of various memory systems. We receive, encode, and store information when we store a memory. The type of information determines how and for how long this information will be stored. Depending on the information, a different sort of memory will be used to store it.

There are three forms of memory, each with its own method of operation, yet they all work together to memorize information. These categories can be thought of as the three processes required for the formation of long-term memory. Long-term memory, short-term memory, and episodic memory are the three forms of memory.

#1 – Sensory memory

Sensory memory is regarded as the earliest level of memory. Sensory memory entails registering massive volumes of information about the environment in a relatively short time. It enables you to retain information received through your senses after the initial input has passed. Sensation refers to the process of receiving information through your senses.

It serves as a buffer for the stimuli received by hearing, seeing, feeling, smelling, and tasting, which are accurately preserved but only for a few seconds. While your senses are responsible for receiving all of these inputs, your perception processes them within your brain. The sensation process refers to the process of the senses receiving all of these stimuli before perceptions may be formed.

The sensory memory is organized into five sensory memory systems:

- Haptic memory (touch)

The haptic memory recalls information initially gathered by the sense of touch. You probably remember how this feels when you think of rain on your face, and this is made feasible by the memory storing such data in the haptic memory.

- Echoic memory (hearing)

The sensory memory that preserves sound is known as echoic memory, also known as auditory memory. You might be able to recall your favorite song as if it were playing right now; this is a memory that was retained after being acquired by the echoic memory.

- Symbolic memory (sight)

The symbolic memory is a sensory memory that preserves visual information after you get it through your vision. Your iconic memory saves information for a few seconds while looking at your screen and reading this text. You probably remember what you see right now if you close your eyes.

- Olfactory memory (smell)

The remembrance of odors is referred to as olfactory memory. You may recall the smell of your favorite food or flower when recalling it, and this memory was stored in your mind by the olfactory memory.

- Gustatory memory (taste)

The gustatory memory is the sensory memory in charge of recalling taste. A lot of information is stored in our memory through our gustatory memory while we are eating or drinking. You probably remember the flavor of your favorite dish since gustatory memory assisted in storing this information in your memory.

#2 - *Short-term memory*

Your short-term memory is in charge of retaining a tiny amount of knowledge for a short period. This information is processed in your short-term memory via sensory memory. This small amount of information is stored in the short-term memory in an active, easily accessible state. The memories preserved in the short-term memory will last approximately 10 to 15 seconds.

Assume you're dialing a phone number and remembering it before dialing it. You read a few numerals, try to memorize them, and enter them. You remember the numerals right now and probably recall them in your thoughts, but you will forget them in the long run. You are employing your short-term memory in this case.

- Working memory

Working memory is a memory system in charge of storing and managing information needed in conjunction with other cognitive skills to complete cognitive activities such as learning and reasoning. Working memory is concerned with memory-in-action; it can remember and apply vital information while engaged in an activity.

- The distinction between short-term and working memory

Both short-term memory and working memory sound very similar; both memory systems maintain information for only a few seconds. The two memory systems, however, are separate. While short-term memory merely stores information, working memory both stores and retrieves data. When doing a task that requires you to recall and accomplish something at the same time, you use your working memory. As an example, you could respond to anything spoken in a current conversation.

#3 - *Long-term retention*

The memory system that maintains information for a longer amount of time is known as long-term memory. This time span can range from a few minutes to a lifetime. Information is transferred to the long-term memory by transferring information in the sensory memory to the short-term memory, which is then retained in the long-term memory. However, not all information will be retained in your long-term memory. Short-term memories may become long-term memories as a result of the repetition process. This indicates that if you rehearse material for a long enough time, it will eventually be stored in your long-term memory. How long this takes depends on what you're attempting to learn and how significant it is to you; it's easier to remember the birthday of someone dear to you than the color of someone's hair you walked past yesterday.

Long-term memory is comprised of the two memory systems listed below:

- Explicit memory

The explicit memory is a conscious thought, which means it's the type of memory you employ while recalling what you did last night or naming sea creatures. The explicit memory is what most people think of when they think about memory. The explicit memory is made up of episodic memory and semantic memory. Personal events, such as a favorite holiday, are stored in episodic memory. The semantic memory stores factual knowledge like a country's capital city or the items on your shopping list.

- Implicit memory

The implicit memory is unconscious; it is what you aren't consciously striving to remember. These memories are unknowingly and accidentally stored. Priming, perceptual, category, emotional, and procedural learning are all made possible through implicit memory.

The procedural memory is part of the implicit memory. Procedural memory is in charge of storing information about accomplishing activities like walking, talking, or riding a bike.

How is memory processed?

Encoding, storage, and retrieval are the three processes involved in remembering information, as previously stated. But how does this connect to sensory memory, short-term memory, and long-term memory? We'll walk through the process of storing a memory, from sensory input to long-term memory.

Stage 1: From sensory memory to environmental input

A memory begins with information detected by the senses. The sensory memory stores information that has been noticed by hearing, seeing, smelling, touching, or tasting. This information will be saved for about a half second before being lost. If the identified information is deemed important enough to be saved, it will be stored in the short-term memory. Otherwise, it will be lost.

Stage 2: Transitioning from sensory memory to short-term memory

It must transform from sensory memory to short-term memory for sensory memory to be preserved for a more extended amount of time. Your short-term memory, like your sensory memory, only remembers information temporarily. If the information in the short-term memory is not processed to the long-term memory, it will be forgotten in roughly 20 to 45 seconds. In contrast to sensory memory, which stores the whole perception of your senses, short-term memory merely stores your interpretation of the information.

The short-term memory capacity is fairly limited; most people can store between five and nine subjects. If these topics are not incorporated into your long-term memory, your brain will often forget them within a minute.

Stage 3: Short-term memory is transferred to long-term memory

Although short-term memories are gone after around 20 to 45 seconds, rehearsal of the knowledge converts them to long-term memory. The information will be encoded by generating judgments and assessments regarding meaning, relevance, and significance of that information. If information is not encoded, it will not be stored in long-term memory.

The knowledge stored in long-term memory can be recovered for an indefinite time. In contrast to short-term memory, long-term memory has an infinite capacity. However, not all information obtained through your senses will reach your long-term memory; in fact, it may not even reach your short-term memory if it is not relevant enough. Even if the information reaches long-term memory, it may be forgotten due to interference or retrieval failure.

Why do we fail to remember?

Even though our long-term memory has an infinite capacity, it is possible to forget information. So forgetting isn't always about losing or wiping information from your long-term memory. We forget for four main causes, which are as follows

Failure to retrieve

Time is one of the most critical aspects of forgetting. Memories that have not been accessed may fade away with time. A memory can be stored and recalled when you learn something new or connect new information with previously stored memories in your brain. These memory traces will begin to go away if this information is not recovered and repeated over time. This is also known as the decay theory, and could be interpreted as a long-ago event that was significant to you. You remember everything about that moment at first, but the specifics start to fade after not thinking about it for years.

Interference

Interference can sometimes cause memories to fade. Some of the memories you have stored in your brain may interfere with other recollections. This can happen when information in your memory is highly similar to other information in your memory. This is often referred to as the interference theory. Perhaps you have a recall of one of your vacations that is actually a memory of another vacation. You can confuse your recollection of these two identical experiences, causing your brain to forget about the original one.

Failure to store

It is possible that memory loss is not caused by forgetting. Sometimes a memory is lost because it never made it into long-term memory at all. This is because encoding frequently fails, preventing information from converting from short- to long-term memory. As in when you're studying from a book, and you thought you understood everything you needed to know for an exam, but then the memory vanishes. Failure to store a memory can be caused by a variety of factors, including a stressful scenario, studying from a book until your memory is overloaded with new knowledge or a lack of focus that you were unaware of.

Motivated forgetting

We sometimes lose a memory because we strive to forget it, for example, when those memories are stressful. Suppression and repression are the two types of actively forgetting memories: Suppression is a conscious kind of memory forgetting, whereas repression is an unconscious form. Perhaps you've been in a stressful or upsetting situation, such as an accident. While you may recall this incident in great detail at first, you may have forgotten the majority of this terrible experience by now.

Other causes of memory loss

Besides forgetting a memory due to the normal forgetting processes of the memory, many reasons can cause memory loss. How these causes might affect the brain or even affect the memory differs per person and situation. Some causes of memory loss are:

- As a result of a brain injury
- Abuse of alcohol
- Brain infections
- Mental illness such as Parkinson
- Low levels of essential nutrients and vitamins
- Overuse of medicines
- Epilepsy

How to improve memory

Is it feasible to improve one's memory? If you've ever forgotten where you put your keys or blanked out material on an important test, you've undoubtedly wished your memory was a little better. Fortunately, there are numerous activities you may engage in to boost your memory.

Obviously, using a reminder system can be beneficial. Setting up an online calendar that sends reminders to your phone will assist you in keeping track of all your appointments and meetings. Making daily to-do lists might help you remember key chores that need to be performed.

But what about all of the critical knowledge that you need to commit to long-term memory? It may take some effort, and it may even necessitate tweaking or drastically altering your typical study schedule, but there are a variety of tactics you can employ to get more out of your memory.

Check out some of these tried-and-true memory-improvement practices before your next big exam. These practical tips will help you improve your memory, recall, and retention of information.

Focus your attention

One of the essential aspects of memory is attention, and you must actively attend to information for it to go from your short-term memory to your long-term memory. Make an effort to study in an environment devoid of distractions such as television, music, and other diversions.

Getting rid of distractions might be difficult, especially if you live with raucous roommates or noisy youngsters. Set aside a little time for yourself.

Request some distance from your housemates or ask your partner to watch the kids for an hour so you can focus on your work.

Structure and organize

Researchers discovered that information in memory is grouped into linked clusters. You can take advantage of this by organizing your study materials. Make an outline of your notes and textbook readings to help you group related themes.

Don't cram

Studying things across many sessions allows you to allow enough time to process knowledge. According to research, students who study regularly recall the content significantly better than those who complete all of their studying in one marathon session.

Visualize concepts

Many people find that visualizing the knowledge they study is really beneficial. Take note of any images, charts, or other illustrations in your textbooks. If you don't have any visual signals, consider making your own. To group related topics in your written study materials, draw charts or figures in the margins of your notes, or use highlighters or pens in different colors.

Making flashcards of various terms you need to remember can sometimes assist in cementing knowledge in your mind.

Use mnemonic devices

Mnemonic devices are a strategy that students frequently employ to aid in recall. A mnemonic is merely a method of remembering information. For example, you might identify a difficult-to-remember term with an everyday item with which you are quite familiar. Mnemonics that use pleasant imagery, comedy, or novelty are the most effective.

Create a rhyme, song, or joke to assist you in recalling a particular piece of information.

Elaborate and practice

Rehearse knowledge to help you remember it better. It would help if you encoded what you are studying into long-term memory to recall it. Elaborative rehearsal is one of the most successful encoding techniques.

Reading the definition of a key term, studying the definition, and then reading a more extensive description of what that term means is an example of this strategy. After a few repetitions of this technique, you should find that recalling the material is considerably easier.

Read aloud

According to research conducted in 2017, reading documents aloud boosts your remember of the material significantly. Educators and psychologists have also observed that having pupils teach new topics to others improves comprehension and retention.

Use this strategy in your studies by instructing a buddy or study partner on new concepts and knowledge.

Relate unknown to known

When studying new material, take the time to consider how this information relates to what you already know. You may substantially boost the likelihood of recalling newly learned information by forming linkages between new ideas and already existing memories.

Vary your study routine

Changing your study habit regularly is another excellent strategy to improve your remember. If you're used to studying in one place, try relocating to a different location during your next study session. If you study in the evening, try spending a few minutes each morning reviewing what you learned the night before.

By incorporating a fresh aspect into your study sessions, you can boost the effectiveness of your efforts and dramatically improve your long-term recall.

Pay special attention to complex information

Have you ever noticed how the material is sometimes easier to remember towards the beginning or conclusion of a chapter? The serial position effect, discovered by researchers, suggests that the order of information can influence recall.

While remembering middle information can be challenging, you can overcome this difficulty by spending extra time rehearsing it. Another approach is to try to restructure what you've learned so that it's simpler to recall. When you come across a particularly tough concept, spend some extra time memorizing it.

Sleep properly

Sleep has long been recognized as vital for memory and learning by researchers. Taking a nap after learning something new has been proved in studies to help you learn faster and recall better. In fact, one 2014 study discovered that sleeping after learning something new causes physical changes in the brain. Sleep-deprived mice grew fewer dendritic spines after completing a learning test than well-rested mice.

So, the next time you're having trouble remembering new knowledge, consider getting a decent night's sleep after you study.

ACCELERATED LEARNING

Understanding how you learn allows you to educate your brain to better retain knowledge and insight. Everything changes once you understand the keys of learning, from how you ask questions to how you consume knowledge. People will believe you have superhuman abilities.

Learning is the process of instilling new information, thoughts, and talents in our minds. We begin learning in the womb and never stop; we are always creating new skills. Every new piece of information we gain adds to what we already know, providing us with a more complete, richer view of the world. And the better our grasp of the world, the easier it is for us to adapt and pivot when our circumstances change.

Biology teaches us that creatures that can adapt to their ever-changing environment survive and thrive. Those who cannot eventually become extinct. The same is true in our personal and professional lives. We've all worked with someone who hasn't kept up with the times, and their unwillingness to stretch themselves and learn something new appears to be causing them to regress.

Because humans don't merely passively acquire new ideas and information, people can end up with a fixed quantity of knowledge. Learning something new necessitates active participation. At FS, we consider learning to be an essential element of our daily work. We improve in order to help you improve, and we provide you with the tools to do so.

What you think you know is the greatest adversary of learning. When you think you know something, discovering something new may force you to reconsider, so it's easy to believe, there's no room for new ideas. However, refusing to modify your viewpoint will keep you in the same location. Overcoming our egos might be one of the most challenging aspects of learning. As a result, being willing to confess when you're incorrect and alter your thinking will help you learn the most. Recognizing your ignorance and deciding to do something about it is the first step toward learning.

I believe that excelling in life necessitates constant lifelong learning. Things change quickly, and you can't rest on your laurels. The optimal method to learn is one that allows you to go to bed a little bit smarter each day.

Why do we fail at learning?

We struggle with learning because we bring a lot of baggage with us—baggage we typically pick up early in life and then struggle to let go of later in life. You can learn considerably more efficiently if you let go of preconceived notions about what you should accomplish. One significant piece of baggage we accumulate is the assumption that we are not learning if we are not visibly active. This is untrue. Learning necessitates reflection time, and it necessitates talking about what you've learned and allowing your thoughts to wander. You must abandon your desire to appear intelligent in favor of attempting to be intelligent.

We struggle with learning because we want it to be simple. We'd all like to find a magic bullet: a quick and easy way to pick up everything we desire and never forget it. The internet is brimming with blog postings boasting that you can learn a language in a week, code in a month, or play the violin overnight. This is just nonsense. Learning is more than merely learning things for one day. It is profound wisdom that enables you to create, invent, and push boundaries.

Another reason we struggle with learning is that the modern environment erodes our attention spans by conditioning us to be constantly distracted. It may seem wonderful at the moment to check your phone for the latest ping, but learning necessitates intense concentration. When you're distracted, new information can't fix itself in your mind, resulting in gaps in your understanding. Focusing is an art—you can design methods that allow you to give your whole attention to whatever you're learning via trial and creativity.

When I talk about rapid learning, I don't mean that you can avoid working hard. We imply that it is possible to identify methods of learning that produce actual results rather than ones that squander time or get you nowhere. However, you must still do the assignment. Learning should be difficult, but it should also be enjoyable.

In fact, when you push yourself to the limits of your abilities, you improve your skills the most. Pushing yourself to the point where it feels difficult but feasible is the core of the intentional practice, a technique used by exceptional professionals in every discipline to improve their competence.

Outside of your intellectual comfort zone is where you will learn the most. As a result, having a lot of helpful guidance early on can be counterproductive if it minimizes the necessary struggle to grasp new content.

If you push yourself beyond your comfort zone, you may fail. In a new field, you may apply new knowledge poorly or misinterpret essential elements of an argument. This is excruciating. It also provides an opportunity to learn from your mistakes. We all dislike looking stupid, but you can't allow failure to stop you from trying to broaden your circle of ability.

Two primary resources for learning

We can learn from two sources: our own experience and history and the experience of others. Exploring the differences between the two can help us choose the best ways to learn from each of them.

Taking lessons from history

By studying history and applying its lessons to the present, you can learn from the mistakes of others. Because history tends to repeat itself, the difficulties and decisions you confront today frequently have historical precedents. Investigating the past teaches us how to shape the future. History is one of the most important sources of essential knowledge for us.

Remember that information decays over time whenever you learn from the past. Much of what you think you know now will turn out to be untrue, just as much of what people thought they understood a century, fifty years, or even a decade ago has turned out to be false. Facts have a half-life, which can be particularly short in domains such as medicine and the social sciences.

It is a folly to believe that we have achieved the pinnacle of human knowledge or that everything you discover now will be true indefinitely. When you learn from history, you draw on lessons influenced by the individual's point of view who recorded what happened. Thus, historical knowledge needs to be updated regularly as you learn from what happened and how you choose to interpret it.

Reflection and learning from experience

Direct experience, in addition to reading, is the primary method we learn.

The process of revising your beliefs and ideas in response to fresh data and experience is known as double-loop learning. You're employing single-loop learning when you continually make the same mistakes, and it won't go you very far. Double-loop learning occurs when you reflect on your experiences, collect new data, and actively seek feedback.

Reflection permits you to turn experience into knowledge. Don't only "do," but also consider what you're doing and what you've done. High achievers make modifications based on their triumphs as well as their mistakes.

About accelerated learning

Accelerated learning is today's most advanced teaching and learning method. It is a complete solution for accelerating and improving both the design and learning processes. Based on the most recent brain research, it has been demonstrated time and again to boost learning effectiveness while saving time and money. Many of today's most influential corporations and educational institutions are reaping the benefits of accelerated learning.

The fact that accelerated learning is based on how we all naturally learn is what makes it so successful. Accelerated learning unlocks a substantial portion of our learning capacity that has been virtually untapped by most traditional learning methods. It accomplishes this by actively incorporating the entire person, employing physical movement, creativity, music, pictures, color, and other ways to engage individuals deeply in their own learning.

Accelerated learning is activity-based and learner-driven, elevating the term "interactive." Instead of having students complete short exercises after instructor presentations, this technique pushes them to discover and create their own knowledge through meaningful activities and authentic experiences that lead to increased learning. The teacher takes on the role of a learning process facilitator, delivering content merely to enhance the learners' process of discovery and creation.

Better learning

We offer the following two tried-and-true methods for boosting your learning.

The Feynman method

If you want to accelerate your learning, the single most effective method we've discovered for grasping new ideas comes from Nobel Prize-winning physicist Richard Feynman. The Feynman Technique ensures that you comprehend what you are taught. It consists of the four steps listed below:

1. Choose a concept that interests you.
2. Pretend you're teaching it to a child—specifically, a sixth-grader. Write it down or express your explanation aloud.
3. Identify gaps in your comprehension that may emerge when attempting to simplify the concept; return to the source material to obtain the information you require.
4. Reread and simplify your explanation.

It works because writing an idea out in a language that a toddler would comprehend forces you to understand it on a deeper level. To hide what we don't understand, we sometimes employ jargon and complex terminology. The Feynman Technique reveals the full scope of our knowledge.

Asking better questions, on the other hand, is a shortcut to faster learning. The most banal questions—those that a sixth-grader could ask—can sometimes educate us the most since they necessitate a detailed response.

How can you tell if you've completely grasped a new idea? Feynman provided a simple alternative test: try to paraphrase it in your own language without using the word "name." For example, without using the word "energy," describe what allows a dog to run.

Repetition at regular intervals

Memorization through rote is ineffective. Period. The key to efficient learning is spaced repetition, a technique that works with your brain's natural retention of knowledge rather than against it.

The process of revisiting knowledge at increasing intervals is known as spaced repetition. This reflects and combats the fact that once you learn something, you eventually forget it, with forgetting occurring quickly at first and then gradually slowing. You use spaced repetition to remind oneself of facts frequently at first, then less frequently.

Memory mastery is achieved by repeated exposure to new content. To learn something, you must recover it from memory again and over again. Retrieval reinforces information retention even more than re-exposure to the original material.

The principles of accelerated learning

1. Learning entails the entire mind and body. Learning is more than just "head" learning (conscious, rational, "left-brained," and verbal), but it also encompasses the entire body/mind, including all of its emotions, sensations, and receptors.

2. Learning is a process of creation, not consumption. Knowledge is something that a learner generates rather than something that a learner consumes. Learning occurs when a student incorporates new knowledge and skills into their existing self-structure. Learning is essentially the process of forming new meanings, neural networks, and electro/chemical interactions patterns inside one's entire brain/body system.

3. Collaboration promotes learning. All excellent learning has a social foundation. We often learn more by connecting with our peers than by any other method. Learning is slowed when students compete with one another. Cooperation among students expedites the process. A true learning community is always preferable to a group of isolated people for learning.

4. Learning occurs on multiple levels at the same time. Learning is not about absorbing one thing at a time in a sequential fashion but about absorbing several things at once. Good learning engages people on multiple levels

simultaneously (conscious and paraconscious, mental and physical) and incorporates all receptors, senses, and pathways into a person's complete brain/body system. After all, the brain is a parallel processor that flourishes when pressed to execute multiple tasks at once.

5. Learning occurs as a result of doing the work (with feedback). People learn best when they are immersed in their surroundings. Things learned in isolation are difficult to recall and quickly fade. We learn to swim by swimming, we learn to manage by managing, we learn to sing by singing, we learn to sell by selling, and we learn to care for customers by caring for customers. The actual and concrete are vastly better teachers than the hypothetical and abstract - as long as there is time for total absorption, feedback, reflection, and reimmersion.

6. Positive emotions improve learning significantly. Feelings influence both the quality and quantity of learning. Negative emotions impede learning. Positive emotions hasten it. Stressful, uncomfortable, and tedious learning cannot compete with joyful, relaxing, and engaging learning.

7. The brain processes information immediately and automatically. The human nervous system is primarily an image processor rather than a word processor. Concrete images are far easier to understand and remember than spoken abstractions. Translating verbal abstractions into

concrete visuals of various types will make those verbal abstractions simpler to learn and retain.

SPEED READING

Reading requires the use of the eyes, hearing, lips, and brain. Because you use your senses and mental capacity more efficiently when speed reading, you activate these senses even more than when reading normally.

What is speed reading?

The following parts explain what happens in your eyes, hearing, lips, and brain while you rapidly read.

Speed reading is seeing

The first step in reading is to see the words. But, when you read, how do you view the words on the page? Before the 1920s, scientists assumed that humans read one word at a time. They assumed that you moved your eyes from left to right across the page as you read, taking in one word after the other. According to this view, rapid readers were those who could identify and recognize words quickly.

Except for novice readers, everyone can see and read more than one word at a time. You move your gaze around the paper in stops and starts, taking in one to five words at a time in rapid glances.

These brief glances serve as a foundation for speed reading:

- Unless you come across words, you don't know or haven't read before, and you read numerous words in a single glance.
- You broaden your eyesight so that you can read and comprehend a large number of words in a single glance.
- You broaden your eyesight to read both vertically and horizontally on the page. Speed readers can read and understand words on two or three separate lines of text in a single glance, in addition to taking in more than one word on a line of text.

Speed reading is sometimes known as silent reading

Because you learned to read using the sound-it-out approach, you utter words to yourself (aloud or in your thoughts) when you read. Your teacher told you in school that you can always read a word by sounding out the letters and letter combinations, and he was correct. For beginning readers, the ability to sound out words is critical.

The disadvantage of the sound-it-out method of reading is that it slows you down. You read at the speed at which you speak, not the speed at which you think. Sounding things out is excellent for beginner readers, but you must eventually abandon sound if you want to be a speed reader. It takes time to say the words, even if you merely mumble them inside your mind.

Saying and hearing words as you read them is referred to as vocalizing in speed-reading terminology. Keep in mind:

- Vocalizing is a relic of your early reading education; you must abandon it if you want to be a fast reader.
- Training yourself to not vocalize while you read is one of the most important speed-reading skills you can gain.

Understanding is achieved through speed reading

The goal of reading is to understand what you read. Your reading speed, vocabulary breadth, and level of familiarity with the topic matter all influence how well you comprehend what you read.

Reading comprehension improves as you read at a faster pace. When you speed read, you can pick up the meaning of words in context since you read numerous words at a time.

Speed reading also has a snowball effect on your vocabulary and general knowledge, increasing your reading speed.

Concentration is required for speed reading

All reading necessitates concentration, even if just for a brief while. On the other hand, speed reading necessitates persistent, intense concentration since speed reading needs you to perform several things at once. To speed read well, you must see and read the words on the page, stay alert to the author's core ideas, think along with the author and detect how she presents the content so you can pin down the essential concepts, and read with more perspective to separate the details from weightier material. To acquire the gist of everything, you must know when to skim, read quickly, and read slowly.

Benefits of speed reading

Speed reading has huge benefits for everyone in everyday life, particularly for business professionals, students, and anyone who reads a lot.

With so much information bombarding us on a daily basis, investing a little time in mastering tactics for rapid reading makes sense. Consider flying through your email in half the time or skimming through your friends' social media posts and responding swiftly.

However, because speed reading tactics require time to learn and you're already busy, you may be thinking why you should bother adding another "must do" item to your To-Do list. Let's take a look at some of the reasons why you should learn to speed read.

1. Self-confidence: you feel at ease in any situation.

Every day, people assess you by the words that come out of your mouth. If you're in a business meeting, you'll be hesitant to present your point of view if you're not confident in your facts. Reading (and understanding what you're reading) provides you with facts that can be converted into knowledge.

You feel at ease with your pals in social circumstances, and they recognize you. However, at parties, you must have something to talk about. And when people are debating a topic, you need to weigh in. Speed reading the news — from world events to gossip — provides you with many ideas for social chit-chat.

2. Money: you will be able to find better employment.

Money represents freedom and security for you and your family. Knowledge is power, whether you desire to advance in your current job or get a better position.

If you want to advance in your career, you must stand out. Online courses and formal advanced education can assist you in accomplishing this. Obtaining a bachelor's or advanced degree makes you more appealing to potential employers in general. Having a degree or qualification that others vying for a promotion do not have raises your value to your employer, and this greater worth translates into a higher income.

Speed reading can help you improve your education by quickly managing all of the coursework required for future education.

3. *Improved personality traits: you'll gain confidence.*

How comfortable are you communicating with your boss? You'll be able to handle their questions if you understand your firm, its competitors, the present market, and financial news. You'll be able to confidently make proposals for your department and the company as a whole. What about expressing your viewpoint to someone you know will disagree with you? Are you sure you want to do that?

If you're well-read, you'll feel comfortable in both situations: learning to speed read is the key.

4. *Improved memory: you'll remember things more easily.*

Speed reading not only makes you a faster reader, but it also improves your comprehension. You'll remember something if you understand why it's significant. Your better memory will benefit you in other aspects of your life as well.

Because memory is a component of creativity, you'll discover that you're more creative in all aspects of your life.

5. More opportunities: you'll improve your learning abilities.

Do you have difficulty focusing on tasks? Speed reading skills can also help you focus. You'll be more engaged in everything you read, and with your increased inventiveness, you'll be motivated to further your education.

More and better prospects arise as a result of your increasing education.

6. Sophistication: your reasoning abilities will increase.

The neuroplasticity of your brain might be affected by speed reading, and it aids in the formation of new neural connections in your brain. This means that not only will your creativity grow, but so your thinking.

7. Feel less stressed because focusing is a meditative technique.

Do you have trouble focusing on tasks? Because information bombards us in so many forms, many individuals attempt to multitask to get more done, resulting in disjointed attention and overall inefficiency. Speed reading teaches you to concentrate, and this, like meditation, relieves tension.

8. Increased ambition: you'll be motivated to advance in your work.

You will become more ambitious if you have a better memory, new inventiveness, increased thinking abilities, and the ability to focus on activities. Your world is expanding, and you'll be eager to advance up the career ladder in your field.

9. Thought leadership: the more you know, the more innovative you can be.

Leaders in any field who are thought leaders innovate. They are creative because they use what they know. They share ideas via cross-pollinating:

Connecting and mixing non-obvious ideas and objects is critical for creativity and a vital component of the creative thinking process. It engages your imagination and hence opens your invention engine, in addition to your ability to reframe difficulties. Tina Seelig

Speed reading could lead you to the next billion-dollar idea — and the ability to put that idea into action.

10. Improved problem-solving abilities.

Everyone faces difficulties, and your subconscious mind can solve them.

If we wanted to compare it to movement speeds, the conscious mind solves issues at a rate of approximately 100–150 miles per hour. Meanwhile, our subconscious is racing at about 100,000 m.p.h. You can stream more information to your subconscious mind by speed reading, and your subconscious can solve your difficulties with new information.

The fastest speed readers in the world

The average adult reading speed is around 200-300 words per minute, but be ready to have your mind blown.

According to the Guinness World Records, Howard Stephen Berg of the United States and Maria Teresa Calderon of the Philippines both claim to be the World's Fastest Reader. They claim to be able to read at speeds ranging from 25,000 to 80,000 words per minute with up to 100% comprehension.

While there is some debate about who holds the official Speed Reading World Record, speed reading records have been established and accepted as authentic.

This seems incredible, but is it even humanly possible?

Let's have a look at some of the world's quickest readers and how they claim to be able to read at lightning speed.

Maria Teresa Calderon

Maria rose to prominence in 1968 after it was reported that she had read a 3,135-word college-level essay in 3.5 seconds.

Not only did she read at a rate of 50,000 words per minute, but she also claimed to have 100% understanding. She was tested numerous times at various colleges to confirm she has this incredible speed reading ability.

She claims to have established a World Record for the fastest reader, reading at 80,000 words per minute with 100% comprehension. While many believe that she still maintains this position, there is no confirmation of an official record to be found.

Maria Calderon went on to make it her life's purpose to "promote reading as a life-changing habit." She claimed to have perfected a technique known as "gestalt" to accomplish these astonishing feats.

To put it as simply as possible, she uses her huge stored knowledge to fill in the gaps as she skims the pages. Her secret to quick reading is mass reading and learning to forecast context by reading important words. While she was famous worldwide for a time, Maria does not appear to be regarded as the world's fastest.

Howard Stephen Berg

There are two names commonly connected with the title of World's Fastest Reader, but most people agree that it belongs to Howard Stephen Berg.

Berg set the Guinness World Record for the World's Fastest Reader in 1990, reading 25,000 words per minute. Even though his claims for words-per-minute are lower than Maria Teresa Calderon's, he did have a confirmed record at one point.

While he was listed as the record holder in the 1990 Guinness Book of World Records, they no longer appear to recognize any fast reading records. This could be because the exact number of words they read is difficult to prove. Some opponents argue that by just pre-reading or remembering the text, speed reading records can be broken.

While his records are not in stone, Mr. Berg's ability to read and learn quickly is widely acknowledged. His advice and teachings are also said to have made a substantial contribution to our knowledge of learning.

So, how does he pull it off?

Berg claims that most of us read with only one voice in our heads and that we should instead approach reading as if we were watching a movie.

He claims that we should cease subvocalizing words in our brains and instead consume information on a page like we do when watching a movie. How do we fully alter how we read and absorb words to simulate watching a movie?

Berg's Speed Reading Test

One of Berg's speed reading exercises may get you started in the right direction, as he believes it can enhance your reading speed by 20% in just a few minutes.

He argues that the power of using your hand to guide your gaze while reading is the key to speed reading. "He reads books by softly stroking their pages," a watcher of one of his YouTube videos reportedly said. In fact, if you observe him in action, you may believe he is absorbing the words with his hands rather than his eyes.

To begin his practice, read a page as you usually would and time yourself for one minute. When you're finished, simply mark your progress with a pencil. Then, for at least ten minutes, practice reading with your hand. You do this by guiding your reading by moving your hand from left to right. Read as quickly as you can comprehend, and if you don't understand what you're reading, slow down a little.

The goal is to become accustomed to utilizing your hand for attention and tempo.

Berg believes that if you test your speed again after this exercise, you will see a considerable boost in speed using your hand.

Speed reading in the modern age

While learning from these great people will help you improve your reading speed, can you read as fast as Maria Teresa Calderon and Howard Stephen Berg?

As you may expect, the majority of research indicates that reading at this extreme speed with any comprehension is highly unlikely. As an example, consider the fastest modern-day readers.

There are numerous speed-reading contests held across the world; however, none of the victors consistently read more than 2,000 words per minute.

Alex Holloway, for example, was the 2018 European Speed Reading Champion. At this competition, each contestant reads the identical book and then has their comprehension rate tested. This champion read 1,700 words per minute and had the highest comprehension rate.

Nobody could read 25,000 - 80,000 words a minute in real life. The finest in the world may be able to piece together general knowledge through skimming, but we all know they aren't getting all of the words. The truth is that they admit to skimming while pretending to have read every word. It's simple: if you're skimming, you're missing words.

However, if you can scan that many words and comprehend a good amount of the meaning, you have accomplished something truly remarkable.

While it is unlikely that you would be able to learn to read every word on a page in a single second, we can learn a lot from studying the world's quickest readers.

START YOUR TRAINING

Unlike certain courses you may have seen promoted in print or on television, the program given in this book does not guarantee that you will be able to read twenty times quicker than you are now in the next month.

There are numerous ways for fast reading, but you will discover the procedures given in this workbook are the simplest to implement. The techniques are entirely natural amplification of your current reading ability, and the exercises help to solve some of the problems frequent issues that impede your ability to read quicker.

As a result of reducing these, you will automatically boost your reading speed if you have trouble. Most students of these approaches will discover that they may boost their reading speed by up to three times in a matter of weeks.

However, as with any course, you must decide on learning how to speed read, and you will have to go through the advised steps.

A few minutes of practice on these exercises each day will greatly speed up your progress.

Everything is kept brief and to the point. Explanations are brief but just enough for you to get the point. The information has been presented in a step-by-step format. Before proceeding, take your time to finish each step to your satisfaction.

By the end of this book, you should be reading - at least - three times faster than before.

A good mindset is the most critical weapon you will have while embarking on any self-improvement quest. You must keep yourself motivated and focused on what you want to do. Learn how to get rid of unwanted influences in your life. Furthermore, a structured physical exercise regimen will tremendously assist in keeping a happy mental state.

Goal setting

It is important to define and work toward an achievable speed reading goal for oneself. Make a commitment to yourself that you will learn to read three times quicker in the following three weeks. There are numerous exercises indicated in the phases that will help you read quicker. You should repeat them as many times as necessary until you are acquainted with the concepts covered in the stage. When you're ready, time yourself and calculate your reading speed. For this, use the timing sheets provided. Also, wherever possible, time yourself on the exercises in the course. This will help you to determine how close you are to reaching your objective and adapt your efforts accordingly. To keep track of your progress, use the timing and assessment sheets included with this workbook. Please review these sheets as soon as possible. The sheets can be found towards the back of the workbook. If necessary, make extra copies of the sheets.

If you discover that you are progressing quicker than you had anticipated, complete your original objective in less time and then rework your goal statement for a faster pace. As an example, suppose you discover that you are reading three times faster at the end of week two than at the end of week three. Reiterate your aim of reading five times faster at the end of week four at the end of the second week. Now get to work on achieving that objective.

Getting ready

The setting for your reading

Before you begin the speed reading strategies on the following pages, consider the setting in which you will be reading. If required, make the necessary changes.

Take this workbook for what it is: a learning tool, not a piece of leisure reading. While reading this workbook, sit at a desk in a comfortable chair. Use a light fixture that is bright and evenly distributed across the surface. Adjust the fixture so that there is no glare and no light hurts your eyes. A more attractive light source than direct light falling on the reading material is indirect light.

To arrange your work environment, use your discretion and these few guidelines. You will require the following materials:

A book for practice - You will need a book to practice your reading. Choose a book of interest to you but that you do not want to read to understand the material. It could be either a novel or a non-fiction book. It should have a type that is of a reasonable size, neither too large nor too little. The type should be legible, and the book should ideally have no images.

You will read this book only for speed reading. While practicing your fast reading, ignore comprehension, and you could even use an already read book.

- A pencil will be used to fill out the worksheets, and it will also function as a pointer.
- A foot ruler is a pointing device that allows you to follow lines in your practice book. Choose a non-transparent one, such as one made of wood.

- You will need a watch to keep track of time, and there must be a second hand.
- A calculator is optional, but it will come in handy for the few calculations you will need to make.

Maintain easy access to all of these materials while working on this course. It's incredibly inconvenient to have to stop what you're doing to locate a pencil because you need to record your most recent accomplishment on a timing sheet. While working on enhancing your reading speed, keep all materials collected in a pocket folder.

Getting your practice book ready

Take some time to prepare your practice book before beginning the course on the following pages. The book's pages should be easy to turn. When you let go of the pages, you're reading, and the book will tend to close if the binding is firm.

Place the book on a flat surface and open it to approximately the middle of the book to loosen the binding. Press down on the book's binding until the book stays open without effort.

Then take half of the pages on either side of the main page and press down on the binding once more. Continue in this manner, turning to approximately half of the pages on all sides of the book. Determine the book's average number of words per line. Count the number of words that appear on ten full lines of printed material. Divide the result by ten. The result should be rounded to the nearest whole number. Fill out the preparation document that comes with this information.

Words in ten full lines equal 110.

The average number of words each line is 110 / 10 = 11 words per line.

Determine the number of lines on each page of the book. Counting the number of lines on a whole printed page of the book is a simple way to accomplish this. Check that the page does not have a few lines missing at the beginning or finish. Now, as indicated below, compute the average number of words per page. Fill out the preparation sheet with your results.

Example: 34 lines per page

11 words per line (from above)

Therefore

Words per page = Lines per page × Words per line

374 words per page = 11 x 34

Understand your current level

Before you begin using speed reading techniques, you need to be aware of your existing ability. You will assess your present reading speed as well as the issues that are preventing you from reading faster.

Once you've grasped this concept, you'll be able to focus on the specific issues you've noticed and work toward diminishing or even eliminating them. To do this, you must know what you are looking for, and knowledge of typical difficulties is beneficial.

Self-evaluation

Before you can track your progress, you must first choose your beginning point. This section will assist you in determining your current reading rate, and you will also evaluate yourself based on how well you perform about the concerns listed below.

Select any two-facing full-page printed pages from your practice book. You will keep track of the time you spend reading these pages. Place the watch in such a way that you can quickly and simply make a mental note of the time. Take a quick look at your watch, noting the start time. Read the pages at a leisurely speed.

Retake note of the time at the end of the second page. This is the end of the world. Record both times on your Start Evaluation form. Fill in the remaining blanks on the sheet. This is the rate at which you are currently reading. This number should be written at the bottom of the document in the space labeled Score A0.

Each of the previously described concerns is also written on the document. They are graded on a scale of 0 to 4.

Consider attentively the processes that occurred through your head when reading the pages for each of the difficulties listed. Now, rate yourself on the scale below and circle the corresponding number on the sheet.

- 0 - must be improved
- 1 - room for improvement
- 2 - acceptable
- 3 - basic standard
- 4 - no such thing exists

Add the circled numbers for each of the problems and write them in the Score B0 space at the bottom of the sheet.

Examine your understanding of the stuff you read. Score yourself again on the 0 to 4 scale above. The number should be circled and written at the bottom of the document in the C0 space.

Scores A0, B0 and C0 are the scores you will use to evaluate yourself as you work through the information on the next pages. They are independent reading-related items that should be evaluated independently of one another. As a result, this course does not utilize a single representative number to assess your reading skills. As your reading skills improve, you should see an improvement in the ratings A, B, and C. As you progress, you will assess your percentage improvement. Several timing sheets are included to help you keep track of your reading pace during practice reading sessions.

You will need to evaluate yourself multiple times on the next pages. The evaluations will provide you with a good idea of your development.

Basic reading issues

• Regression

Regression is the act of re-reading when your eyes make an error in following lines or words in a line. In some circumstances, your eyes may return to the same line, but in others, you may discover that you have missed a few lines because your eyes traveled too far down. In any event, the outcome is that you must refocus your attention and re-read the text, decreasing your reading pace.

As a fast reader, you will almost certainly avoid this issue. This problem is easily solved by employing pointing devices such as a ruler or your fingertips.

• Reading word-for-word

We have been trained to read one word at a time since the beginning of school. You began at the beginning of the line and read each word one at a time until you concluded. Then you began reading the line immediately following the one you had just done, one word at a time, starting with the line immediately following the one you had just finished. Most likely, you never modified your reading style and continue to read one word at a time.

As a rapid reader, you will alter your reading style. You'll start seeing words as groups rather than individual words, and you'll learn to extract meaning from the groups of words you perceive. For obvious reasons, this procedure is much faster.

• Reading aloud and pronouncing words

This is the other issue that has most likely plagued you when you first learned to read. When you first learned to read, you probably said the words out as you read them. Your teacher taught you to read the word dog, for example, by saying each letter, d, o, g, and then speaking the word dog itself aloud. When you moved to read silently to yourself, you internalized the method that was taught to you. You began to mentally speak the words that you had read to yourself. This is referred to as vocalization, or the process of lending sounds to what is being read. It is vital to pronounce the words while learning to read since it helps you connect the object and the word that represents it. However, after your reading skills have advanced beyond the first few years of school, vocalization is no longer required for comprehension and is a big factor slowing you down.

When you see a dog in the park, for example, you do not need to pronounce the word "dog" to yourself to realize that the animal you are looking at is a dog. That information is automatically retrieved from your memory. However, even if you read the word "dog" in print, you will find yourself pronouncing it in your head.

You will learn to minimize the problem of vocalization as a speed reader. You'll start to see words as images. You will very certainly never be able to eradicate vocalization, and you will frequently employ it when encountering an unknown term. This naturally leads us to the next issue that the average reader will encounter.

- A lack of vocabulary

You could be one of the many readers who are constrained by their existing vocabulary. This, in turn, slows down your reading pace. When you come across a new word, you have no choice but to look it up in a dictionary. Many readers, however, simply skip the term and continue reading, jeopardizing their comprehension of the subject. By doing so, individuals miss out on the opportunity to learn a word and commit it to memory by linking it to the context in which they were reading it. One of the most effective ways to improve your vocabulary is to tie a new term to the context in which you encountered it.

Many authors will tell you that knowing the constructs, common prefixes, and suffixes found in the language is a powerful approach of acquiring new words and expanding your vocabulary. Using word lists is another excellent way to increase your word power. Each word is accompanied by a sentence in which it is used. After reading this statement, you must write your sentence using the same word. Working through one of the books that help develop vocabulary is highly advised if you find yourself limited by your word power.

If you have a large enough vocabulary, you can guess the meaning of an unknown word from the context in which it appears. When paired with speed reading, this strategy becomes extremely effective, allowing you to continue reading without losing the sentence's meaning.

- Inability to concentrate

There is frequently a lack of focus on the subject that you are reading. When you come to the end of the paragraph, you realize you have no idea what you just read. Regardless of how strong your IQ or memory is, you will not understand what you are reading and will not recall the material if your mind is not on it.

This problem arises primarily because you are not using your brain to its full potential. As a result, your brain seeks other, unrelated distractions. As a result, you lose concentrate on your reading content. Many academics estimate that we only employ 10% of our brain power. When you speed read, you use more of your available brain power to read. Because your mind will be busier, it will wander considerably less than it did previously. This has the added benefit of increasing comprehension and retention of the material read.

SPEED READING TECHNIQUES

While most people feel that developing a habit of speed reading is tough, the truth is that it is an art that can be learned with the correct set of exercises and tools.

With a little experience, you'll discover that it's straightforward to breeze through a dozen pages in a matter of minutes. While I'm not the fastest reader in the world, I've discovered that boosting my speed-reading ability has flipped a switch in my brain that has had a long-lasting effect on every aspect of my life.

More importantly, I believe it is a valuable talent for everyone interested in personal growth. Consider the following:

- Consider the one book that has had the greatest influence on your life.

- Consider how your life would have been different if you hadn't read it.

When you learn how to speed read, you substantially enhance your chances of discovering the next great book. Imagine being able to read ten, twenty, or thirty more books this year without having to devote large sections of your day to paging through them.

If it just takes one book to change a life, thirty books could convert you into someone you never believed you could be.

You can read with no loss if you discover how to boost both your reading speed and understanding. This is critical since you do not want to enhance your reading speed, but the stuff you read leaves an impression.

The 9-step method for reading faster

When it comes to reading speed, your eyes and mind are the two most significant instruments. Your eyes see the words, and your mind processes the phrases.

Unfortunately, most people never push their eyes or minds to their limits. Instead, they learned to read at an early age, gradually improved their talent over time, and never considered that there was a way to teach themselves to read quicker.

We consciously know that we want to prepare to the best of our ability in the military, higher education, operating rooms, and life-or-death circumstances. If reading a book can change our lives, why wouldn't we want to read well?

To fast read, you must pay attention to what your eyes are doing while reading. To read a sentence, your eyes must shift from left to right. That portion is straightforward, but many people appear to overlook the idea that they can teach their eyes to move faster. Simply looking at a text and scanning it from left to right as soon as possible would exercise the muscle that controls your eyes.

As a result, the first step in becoming a speed reader is to comprehend that our eyes get faster and more prepared to read quickly by exercising and practicing with this scanning motion. It's similar to working out a muscle; it will develop stronger if you do it consistently. Unfortunately, it is most likely not how your eyes work right now.

What's most likely happening is that as you read, you occasionally dart back to the left or skip ahead slightly, requiring you to readjust your eyes. There is no movement. More significantly, you almost certainly never try to accelerate the movement of your eyes.

The idea is to acquire a few new habits that will allow you to learn the skill swiftly, easily, and enjoyably. After that, the rest is a piece of cake.

Let's get started with the nine-step process!

1. *Master the art of reading without subvocalizing*

Welcome to the most vital and challenging habit to break. When it comes to developing a reading habit, we are frequently constrained by the time it takes our subconscious mind to pronounce the words on the page. We don't utter them out loud, but our minds do: this is referred to as "subvocalizing."

When we utter a word out loud, it takes some time to pronounce it. When we read, however, we do not need to pronounce the words. We can just absorb them. Have you ever caught yourself quietly reading a text while your lips imitated what it would be like to utter the word out loud? That is called subvocalization.

Unfortunately, the practice of saying words as we read them is so firmly ingrained in our unconscious minds that breaking free from it appears impossible.

A fantastic trick is to pick any word in this text and stare at it for a few seconds in complete quiet. There will still be some sub-vocalization, but by simply monitoring words without using your internal voice to pronounce them, the new habit will begin to establish on its own.

An excellent way to avoid this phase is to begin looking at and thinking about words without speaking them. This section may appear obscure or abstract at first, which is completely acceptable. All you need to worry about is gazing at words without wanting to hear how they sound.

After a few hundred words of practice, you'll notice a difference between using the voice in your brain and simply allowing it to enter your consciousness. And once that's done, you've removed the main impediment to quick reading. It may not be easy at first, but once you've mastered this section, everything else will be a piece of cake.

2. Establish Your Current Baseline

Another important aspect of speed reading is the capacity to recognize your own progress. A baseline is required before you can quantify your progress. Once you've established a baseline, you'll need to compare your readings to it regularly.

ReadingSoft.com is an excellent resource for tracking your performance because it provides a quick, reliable measurement of how quickly you're reading. By taking the tests here on a regular basis, you'll find it much easier to notice that you're progressing, which will provide you with all the motivation you'll need to keep going.

The difficulty with recognizing your own baseline is that it's difficult to translate it into practical terms when a program claims you're reading a certain number of words per minute. It's a good place to start, but from a practical standpoint, knowing how long it takes to read an average page is more crucial. If the average person takes 5 to 10 minutes on each page, a speed reader just needs 2 or 3 minutes. This indicates that a 200-page book will take a speed reader 400 minutes and an ordinary reader 1,000 to 2,000 minutes. That means the average reader will have to devote an additional 13 hours to the same book. That's more than a half-worth day of missed time!

However, it is not as simple as going from a 17-hour reader to a speed reader. There will be numerous barriers in your path, but fortunately, most of them are easily overcome.

3. *Make use of a pointer, an indicator, or your index finger.*

When reading, using your finger to guide oneself is frequently thought to be reserved for children and then forgotten once they've mastered the skill. This approach, however, comes in helpful again when learning to fast read for a few essential reasons.

The most difficult and time-consuming challenge in fast reading is not developing new skills but deleting old ones that operate against us. One of these skills that works against us is our preference for reading without a guide, yet utilizing a guide is essential to learn as quickly as possible. It is unquestionably non-negotiable.

If you were to watch me fast read, you'd see that I don't require a guide and that my eyes are continuously jumping from the beginning to the finish of the line. What you might not realize is that I'm moving at a pretty constant pace.

In other words, the amount of time it takes me to cross a single line of text is largely constant as I move down the page. The only exception is when I experience insight or become confused while reading, but these are both natural parts of the process.

The basic purpose of utilizing a guide is to move the guide at a highly consistent speed. You should not stop or slow down your finger. It should just go from one side of the text to the other at a highly consistent speed, requiring you to move your eyes to keep up. By exercising in this manner, you will be able to detect when you become stuck or lose momentum far more easily than if you simply tried to follow behind and advance as rapidly as possible.

You can't maintain a fluid and flowing style of speed-reading if you only strive to move swiftly because you'll ultimately hit your limit and skip a word. This leads to backtracking, and backtracking leads to confusion.

If you repeat this process twice per page, you could easily add 30 seconds to each page or 100 minutes to a 200-page book. Throughout a book, that's an extra hour and a half lost to retracing. You must train yourself to view fast reading as a marathon rather than a race.

4. Concentrate on control

Moving through text, you will notice that certain book sections are easy to read, while others are too dense with essential information to read fast. This is a natural reading component, and seamlessly moving from dense subject to easy reading is a sign of control. Remember that speed isn't the only significant aspect of speed reading: you must also read.

Let's look at two different books to demonstrate this concept.

The first book will be a dense, monotonous history textbook. If we needed to find specific dates and names within the book, we could simply go through the pages quickly while scanning for the names. If we wanted to understand the significance of these persons and dates, we would have to slow down and pay closer attention to the material.

Our second book is a work of fiction. It's a colorful tale of a family imprisoned on a mountain and their adventures attempting to find their way out.

Because our brain appreciates the book, there is no real reason to control the reading process unless we don't grasp a particular aspect of the story. We may simply read the material quickly, allowing the story to fill our minds, and then slow down when we feel we have missed anything important.

In this view, the ramifications of rapid reading for diverse texts are evident. The novice makes the mistake of thinking that speed reading is all about speed, but it is basically about reading. The ability to manage one component of how we read is referred to as speed.

5. Teach your eyes to move slowly

Recognizing how much your eyes move when reading is one of the most important and most accessible epiphanies you will have on your way to becoming a speed reader.

The ordinary person's eyes cannot move in a single, flowing line without having to backtrack. Things enter our peripheral vision and divert our attention. If you start paying attention to your eyes, I guarantee you'll notice how often you move back, then forward, then back again, with less distraction.

In the long term, this movement can add hours to your reading experience and may prohibit you from finishing at all.

Train your eyes without the use of a book

A fantastic non-book exercise is to practice moving your eyes from left to right while also moving your head from left to right. Make sure to keep your eyes forward as you go. Your head should move while your eyes remain static. After a few repetitions of staring from left to right, repeat the exercise, but this time allow your eyes to travel with the motion of your head. Your gaze should remain concentrated and not shift to the left or right. Finally, maintain your head straight and take a couple of glances to the left and right. Your head should be completely aligned as you cast a horizontal line to the left and right.

You've just identified all of the essential components of using your eyes to speed read by doing these exercises. There is a motion made by the head that is not shared with the eyes, motion created by the eyes that is shared with the head, and motion created by the eyes that is not shared with the head.

Keeping your eyes locked in position, as in the first exercise, aids with focusing on a particular word or phrase that you may choose to read slowly. Moving your eyes with your head, as in the second sentence, aids in the creation of a calm and flowing motion as you move from line to line or page to page. The essence of scanning from one side of the line to the next is moving your eyes independently, as seen in the third exercise.

You will be able to easily manipulate your eyes over the page at speeds you never imagined were possible by teaching your eyes to scan in straight lines and using the motion of your head to add that extra layer of control to the mix.

6. Omit minor, unimportant words

To comprehend how speed readers can move through pages so quickly, it's critical to recognize that not all words are created equal. There are a lot of small, cryptic words that don't help you, and forcing yourself to read them will just make things worse.

A good illustration of this is written out in the very first tip. The article provides an outstanding example text that demonstrates how certain words do not assist significantly in understanding what the phrase is saying.

If we return to our previous understanding that an extra thirty seconds each page can translate to an hour and a half, imagine what can be accomplished if we eliminate all of the "if," "is," "to," "the," and other small-yet-insignificant words. It is based on the same notion of saving time, but it requires a whole different skill set to master.

The nicest part about skipping the short words is that they add nothing beneficial to your reading experience, thus skipping them effectively means that you get more out of your reading experience. Isn't it cool? We're gaining more by skipping words. Take a moment to absorb that.

It's as simple as understanding that you don't need to pay attention to the small words to train yourself to skip them. Allow your eyes to continue traveling across the irrelevant words.

Your brain will automatically learn to skip over them for you over time, and you will be able to scan phrases while skipping a large amount of insignificance.

7. Experiment with powerful woftware

Simple, common apps that expedite the process of learning the skill are the ideal resources for speed reading practice. There are several options to select from, and the majority of them have fantastic features that make using them both an exercise in speed reading, and a means to save time.

Accelerator is an iOS software that lets you import articles, documents, and other materials, as well as links, into a speed-reading practice tool. Its effectiveness as a practice tool and a learning tool doubles because it includes articles you'll already like to read, so the exercise doesn't feel tedious or mechanical. Instead, it feels like you're reading an article while practicing your speed reading. Therefore, Accelerator is strongly advised.

Spreeder is another excellent application for copying and pasting anything into a little word processor. The software then converts everything you've already pasted into its own workout, allowing you to pick and select exactly what you'd like to read and practice on, all within the same app. It's an excellent choice for individuals who want to gain a lot of value without spending a dime.

Spritz is a little different from some of these apps because it does not teach us how to read quicker; instead, it teaches us how to utilize its software to reconfigure what we want to read in a completely new way. The key to Spritz reading is to not move your eyes, and it flashes the text in front of your eyes, emphasizing one letter to center each word and keeping your eyes tracking the words as they pass at what appears to be light speed.

I've only tried it with the Spritz demo. Nonetheless, even at a blistering 700 words per minute, I found myself perfectly comprehending the content. However, if you read a complete book's worth of material, this reading may become tiresome. In my opinion, Spritz is unquestionably one of the more intriguing speed reading applications.

ReadMe! is an excellent choice for individuals who own an eReader. This program has a lot of features, but it's primarily meant to help with speed reading via ebooks. Because modern technology has made ebooks one of the most convenient reading methods, this one is highly recommended for all ages, from children to professionals.

Finally, Acceleread is a fast reading tool swiss army knife. While the majority of the other applications on this list have import capabilities or work with specific types of text, Acceleread is a true-blue speed reading trainer with its exercises. The purpose of this one is to focus on the exercises themselves in order to accelerate growth, rather than importing literature that you would want to read and forcing you to practice with it. This is similar to going to the gym for speed reading.

8. Practice text scanning and skimming

You've probably heard most of what you need to know by this time. That's correct, and you already have the fundamental skills required to begin speed reading.

Practice, on the other hand, does make perfect. To develop this valuable ability, you must first become accustomed to skimming through pages and pages of text. The skill will come slowly at first, but it will certainly become easier after a few days. You'll be better in five weeks than you are today, so sit back and enjoy the journey; you'll get there in the end.

In the next pages, you will find some exercises designed to show you the importance of speed reading training. Just keep in mind that practice makes perfect, and the time it takes to grow will fly by.

9. Keep practicing and timing yourself

Congratulations if you've made it this far: you now have everything you need to handle this on your own. It may appear like fast reading is a very tough skill to learn, but it isn't. It only takes a few essential concepts and a lot of practice.

At this point, your major goal should be to time yourself regularly and continue to practice the skills mentioned in this article.

Consider saving this for future reference, and return every now and then to review the page and see if there's anything you missed the first time.

Practical tips to increase your reading speed

Put an end to your inner monologue

The inner monologue, also known as subvocalization, is a very prevalent characteristic among readers. It is the process of reciting the words in your brain while you read, and it is the most significant impediment to increasing your reading speed.

Don't be concerned if you hear voices in your brain while reading. You're alright as long as it's your own voice reading along with you. In fact, this is how teachers educate children to read: pronounce the words silently in their heads while they read.

Do you recall hearing the phrase "Read in your brain as I read the passage aloud" quite frequently in the classroom? As a young reader, this habit of having an inner monologue was instilled in you in this way.

When you first learned to read, you were taught to sound out every word and read aloud. When you were well enough, your teacher had you start reciting the words in your head. This is how the habit began, and most people continue to read in this manner, and it has no negative impact on them until they begin to want to read at a faster pace. If you want to improve your reading speed, this is the first hurdle you must overcome.

Why is this bothering you? The average reading pace is roughly equal to the average talking speed, and the average adult reading speed, according to Forbes, is 300 words per minute. The average speaking rate is the same.

Because most individuals read by pronouncing the words aloud in their heads, they tend to read at the same rate as they talk. This means that if you keep up your inner monologue, your reading speed will only grow so much. If you want to keep improving your reading speed, you must get rid of it. To do so, you must first recognize that it is useless. You don't have to say every word in your brain to understand what you're reading. When you were younger, you could input the meaning simply by viewing the words, and your brain is still processing the information.

Do you, for example, stop to speak the word "YIELD" in your brain when you see a "YIELD" sign? Obviously not, and you simply gaze at it, and it processes itself. This is what you should do when reading print material, such as books or paperwork.

Try reading while listening to instrumental music through headphones or chewing on some gum if you're having trouble with this. A distraction will keep your brain from focusing on subvocalization, but you will still glance at and comprehend the words.

Word-Crunching

The concept of word-chunking is strongly related to the concept of eliminating the inner monologue. This is the act of reading numerous words simultaneously, and it is essential for reading quicker. Although all of these reading methods are related, word-chunking is perhaps the most active strategy to utilize when working to improve your reading speed.

Even if we are conditioned – as discussed with the inner monologue – to read each word at a time and not miss a single article, a person can take in numerous words at a time. One approach to make this step easier is to use your peripheral vision, but we'll get to that in the next part.

For the time being, concentrate on reading three words at one glance. Continue down the page in this manner, noting how much faster you finish the entire page of text. You can still analyze and grasp what you read, but it takes much less time.

Now, take that idea a step further. Draw two vertical, parallel lines down your page with a pencil to divide the text into three sections. As usual, begin at the top left of the page and cover anything below that line with your hand or a piece of paper. Concentrate on reading the text in each segment as a separate entity. Combine the words and read them at a glance, as you would a road sign. Continue doing this down the page, adjusting the paper as needed. You will see that your speed has increased.

Continue using this strategy until you feel confident enough to push yourself a little further.

Do not read the words on the page again

Before we get to the portion about peripheral vision – the real kicker – you'll want to stop the habit of rereading the text on the page.

If you observe the average person's eyes while reading, you will see that they bounce and flicker around, and they do not flow back and forth equally as they should. This is because the ordinary person – and you, too – tends to go back over words they have already read. This is one factor preventing you from increasing your reading speed. You most likely do this without even realizing it, making it a difficult habit to quit. Even if it may feel a little juvenile, the simplest method is to use your finger or a bookmark to help you along.

Continue to move your finger over the page without pausing or going back. As your finger moves along the text, continue to monitor the words. Consider what you've read when you've finished. You didn't go back over a single word (I hope!), but you remember what you read.

Use your peripheral vision

Congratulations! You've arrived at the crucial stage that links everything together. While this is not the final stage, it is unquestionably the most important.

Use the techniques described above to view and interpret many words at the same time. Instead of chunking words into smaller chunks, try reading one line at a time. This entails staring at the center of the line and reading the remainder of it using your peripheral vision. Scanning the page in this manner will reveal that you not only understand what you read, but you did it in record time.

Utilize a timer

Speaking of 'record time,' this is your chance to put yourself to the test and focus on improving your reading speed each time you read. Set a timer for one minute and normally read as the time passes. When the timer runs off, keep track of how many pages you've read. WordstoPages.com will assist you in determining how many words you have read. Now, put everything you've learned together and retake the test. Make a note of that number as well.

Continue repeating this, beating your previous count each time. Set a daily or weekly goal for yourself and reward yourself when you achieve it. Continue playing this short game, and you'll be able to speed up your reading in no time!

Establish a goal

Holding yourself accountable can help you stick to your reading and timer testing. Set a goal for yourself to read a specific number of pages every day/week/etc., and adhere to it. When you've reached it, reward yourself. Anyone can benefit from an incentive!

Read more

"Practice makes perfect," as the old adage goes, is actually very accurate. Any professional, artist, musician, or other creative person practices their craft regularly. The reader should do the same thing. The more you read, the better you will become. The more proficient you are at reading, the faster you will read.

Before breakfast, Theodore Roosevelt read one book, followed by three or four more in the evening. He also read papers and pamphlet-style reading material. I'm not sure how long these books were, but I assume they were about the average length. Use his obsession to fuel your ambition.

Use a marker

As you read, do you notice your gaze slipping and sliding across the page? It's not a problem. Place an index card beneath each line and slide it down as you read. This will keep you focused on reading one paragraph at a time, rather than darting your eyes about and taking in nothing.

Practice expanding your vocabulary

Consider this: You're reading along when you come across a word you don't recognize. Do you avoid it? Do you try to deduce it from the context? Do you take the time to look it up? Whichever path you select, you are greatly slowing down, if not completely stopping, your time to seek up the retarding word.

You will know more words if you work on growing your vocabulary. The more words you have in your vocabulary, the faster you will read. The more you can read, the faster you can read. It may seem self-evident, yet it is significant.

FIRST, skim the main points

Finally, if you're in a genuine hurry and need to read something by yesterday, take a deep breath and relax. Open the book and spend some time going over the main ideas. Check out the table of contents. Check out the subtitles, and read the captions that appear behind the diagrams. Get a general sense of the chapter/section/etc.

Then, for each main segment, read the first paragraph. Read the final paragraph. Read on to the center. Think about it and piece it together in your brain. Then, using the principles we just described, begin reading everything else. You'll retain more information and finish your reading more quickly.

In conclusion, the next time you need to read anything quickly, tell yourself, "Shut up and look at the page!"

How to measure your reading speed

The first step in effectively measuring your reading speed is to recognize that the majority of the reading material you encounter will generally fall into three content categories:

- Easy-to-read material
- Medium-level reading material
- Difficult-to-read material

If you want to precisely test your reading speed, you should do so for each of the three difficulty levels that you read (easy, medium & difficult). This will offer you with a "reading range," which will provide a more accurate assessment of your reading speed. For example, you may read easy stuff at 300 words per minute (wpm), medium-level information at 200 wpm, and difficult material at 100 wpm.

What if you could double your speed? How much more of this material could you get through each day, and how much more free time would you have?

What types of reading materials should you use?

You should begin by testing your reading speed with medium-level content. This is most likely the content you read the most frequently as part of your daily reading regimen. This includes general news, blog articles, and magazine stuff (Perfect Examples: Wall Street Journal, Entrepreneur Magazine, New York Times, or The Economist). This category would also include best-selling fiction and non-fiction.

Simply read for one minute and count how many words you read in that one minute to determine your reading speed. This is your reading speed in "words per minute" (wpm).

If you don't want to count every single word, you can estimate your reading speed by counting the number of lines you read and multiplying that number by the average amount of words each line.

After you have measured your reading speed in medium-level content, you should measure it again in easy stuff. Light fiction or nonfiction, general news, comics, children's books, and anything else that appears to be simple reading to you would be deemed easy material. This type of material is typically read at a faster rate than medium-level content. In this type of literature, measure your reading speed once again.

Now that you've determined your reading speed in medium-level and easy stuff, you'll want to determine your reading speed in more challenging material. This will give you a more accurate picture of your reading speed across different sorts of information.

Difficult reading would be complex, technical content. Philosophy, the sciences, textbooks, work materials, and industry, trade, or academic periodicals are all examples. This would also include the material that takes the greatest time and requires the most concentration from you as a reader. This may also include the majority of what you read for school or work.

Calculate your reading speed for this challenging content. You can now be assured that you have tested your reading speed in the most broad way possible across all forms of reading that you may conduct.

These three reading rates have now become your personal standards, which we want you to surpass. It makes no difference how low or high they are. All that counts is that you improve. Before moving on to the next suggestion, make a note of your reading speed in easy, medium, and tough content. Make a record of your outcomes so you can track your development in the future.

TRAINING EXERCISES

Reading speed is approximately 200 words per minute on average. If you pushed someone reading 200 words per minute to read at 250 words per minute, which is 50 words per minute faster, they would most likely have the same level of comprehension. Why is this the case? The truth is that when you go a little faster, you force yourself to focus more.

One idea behind enhancing your reading speed is to force yourself to go a little quicker than usual. This idea of pushing yourself to make changes and going outside of your comfort zone is similar to other things in life where you try to improve. Assume you're attempting to learn to perform a sport or an instrument. If you have a coach, they will push you to go faster and urge you to step beyond your comfort zone. At the same time, they will encourage you to improve.

Simple speed reading test

Pushing ourselves beyond our comfort zones is how we improve in anything. I'd like you to consider your current reading pace. What if you just pushed yourself a little harder? What level of comprehension might you achieve?

I want you to put this to the test. Perform a workout and practice on your own because the only way to improve is to put in the effort and practice. So I really, really want you to do this. I'd like you to set aside some time for me. I want you to try to read through the information a little faster than usual. Don't be afraid. Consider this exercise so that it's not a huge issue; it's just practice. I want you to give it a shot and see what happens. For around 15 minutes, read. Take some current work you're working on, whether it's a novel, a textbook, work-related material, or anything else. I'd like you to try reading it a little faster than usual.

Some of you will discover that moving a little quicker can really increase your focus. Think of it this way: when you move faster, you force your mind to keep up. When you put your intellect to the test to keep up, you'll naturally focus a little more. You will not only have a little more speed, but you will also have better comprehension if you do this.

Consider it in the same way as you would when driving. You're more concentrated if you're going down the highway at 70 miles per hour, right? It is due to the fact that if you make one mistake, your life is jeopardized. What if you're only going 5 miles per hour? How much concentration do you need if you're just traveling 5 miles per hour? I think we can all agree that you don't have to concentrate as hard if you're traveling 70 miles per hour.

Sometimes the increase in pace is what allows you to focus more. This is a simple thing you may do to teach and train yourself to read quicker. Experiment with going a little faster than usual. Experiment with stepping outside of your comfort zone. Allow 15 minutes. Attempt to read in this manner. Try going a little faster than usual, or whatever seems comfortable. Push yourself a little bit harder. See how far you can get with your understanding. Consider it entirely an experiment. You might want to give it a shot for 15 minutes.

Here are some suggestions that you might wish to try. Maybe you read for 5 minutes at a time. After the 5 minutes are up, give yourself a score ranging from 0 to 100 percent for your comprehension during that time. Then, after another 5 minutes of reading, give yourself another assessment of your comprehension.

Obviously, estimating your comprehension is not a true score for your comprehension but rather a self-analysis. The entire goal of this is to obtain that self-analysis and see how much comprehension you can truly acquire if you go a little faster than usual. As you might expect, the more you practice doing this, the more you push yourself outside of your comfort zone, the better you'll get. Try it out. Set aside 10-15 minutes and try to proceed a little faster than you normally would through a subject that you have to read.

Example of speed reading drill

Learning to read faster needs practice, and just like any other ability, there are drills and exercises you can perform to improve your reading skills. The fundamental "speed drill" is one exercise that can be beneficial to practice. Reading Speed drills help you increase your reading speed by forcing you to see words at a faster rate than you normally do.

Make sure you have calculated your current reading speed before beginning the following drill. Here's a simple example of a speed drill.

Step #1

Use material that you are accustomed to reading. Books, such as fiction or nonfiction, newspapers or magazines, blog postings, textbooks, and so on.

Step #2

Read for 10 minutes. Don't go any faster or slower than usual. Read aloud to improve your understanding.

Step #3

Make a note of where you stopped after 10 minutes of reading.

Step #4

Return to the beginning, where you began, and try reading the same stuff again but in less time (6 minutes).

The idea is to see words quickly. And the simplest method to do it is to go over content you've already read. This is your very first "speed drill." You simply want to go over the same topic again in 6 minutes. Don't worry if it seems a little too quick; the idea is to become acclimated to seeing words at a much faster rate. While performing this exercise, make sure to use your hand, finger, or pen as a reference.

Step #5

Return to the beginning (where you originally started reading for the first 10 minutes). Complete the content in 5 minutes. Remember that you aim to read faster than you typically would, even if it means sacrificing understanding.

Step #6

Return to the beginning. Complete the content in 4 minutes. This is the final "speed drill."

Step #7

You just got done with 15 minutes of "speed drills." You should now recalculate your reading speed. Find some fresh reading material. You can either pick up where you left off in the first 10 minutes of reading, or you can choose different stuff. Just make sure it's the same level of difficulty. Read for 1 minute to ensure proper understanding; make sure you're reading normally right now. After you've finished reading, compute your reading speed. At this moment, the majority of people are improving their reading speed.

That's fantastic if you improve! We'll strive to build on it in the future. Don't worry if you don't. With practice, you'll get better. This drill should ideally be practiced for two weeks, 15 minutes every day.

Reading comprehension exercises – Skimming and scanning

Here are some hints and tips to help you succeed when you have to complete reading comprehension assignments in a short amount of time. Time yourself at each step and make a record of your marks so you can see how far you've come.

The more you read a text, the more you will understand it. Just keep your Spanish in mind when you read challenging texts, and the Onion Approach is essential. You must read your content at least three times, each time focusing on a different aspect, as indicated below.

In Reading Comprehension exercises, there are two sorts of questions: Skimming Questions and Open-Ended Questions. They assess your overall comprehension of the material, such as the topic, the major concepts, and the point in this or that section or the entire text. You will not be able to answer these questions correctly if you skip Steps 1 and 2 below, unless the material is extremely simple for you. Scanning Questions are the other type. These do not necessitate a broad grasp. They want you to locate the exact information requested, such as a specific quantity or a specific term.

Although you may choose to skip any sections of this technique in the exam, please follow all of the procedures for the time being, until you have enough practice and are proficient in this approach. The method is more useful when the text is challenging. However, in order to learn the approach, you must also utilize it with easy-to-understand literature.

#1

Skim (read quickly) the title, directions, and comprehension questions, underlining (very quickly) key words. This underlining/comprehension activity will be completed in Step 3.

#2

Read the text quickly (for, say, 750 words, it should take you about 3 minutes - you can only achieve this mark if you practice a lot, so remember it is a process, and write down your marks so you can notice your progress). You should identify the following during your skimming:

- the type of text (different texts organize information differently, e.g. a news item has the important information at the beginning, in an essay you can find it in every topic sentence at the beginning of paragraphs, and if we know about that, we can be quicker finding the info we need)
- the subject
- the approach to the major thesis

If you can recognize other things, i.e. understand more, that's fantastic. However, keep in mind what was discussed previously.

<u>Some tips for skimming well!</u>

Skimming through the written language is like jumping from one stepping stone to the next! You don't have to read every word, for example, in examples or chunks that you know are developing themes described in the topic sentence. You should pay more attention to the beginning and ending sentences in the text and paragraphs since those sentences usually tell you what the paragraph's focus is. You should pay closer attention to what appear to be essential terms, such as words from the same universe (semantic field) as the issue. The title and the introduction are vital to pay attention to since they provide information about the topic and the tone. They are necessary to grasp the overall concept. The ending, too, but the text may not be complete, so we can't always rely on it (take note!). Then, suppose it's an essay or article. In that case, there will be topic sentences (what the paragraph is about) at the beginning of paragraphs and a kind of finishing sentence or introduction to the next point in the following paragraph at the conclusion.

#3

Take a second look at your questions. A quick and cautious examination, and if they are tough to understand, take your time, making it less rapid but just as careful! Underline essential terms so that when your eyes move from the text to the questions, they can discover the area where they need to stop! If you have a question with options and the answers appear to be all true, figure out where the difference is because you need to choose the best option.

#4

Slowly and carefully read. Allow yourself plenty of time. Even if you don't plan to, you will develop speed with practice. (Remember to keep track of how long each process takes you.) Keep track of which sections you comprehend well and which appear to be tough. Read them all carefully and attempt to comprehend them, but don't spend your entire life on the harder ones because you'll return to them in your second scanning. (This is why we perform a second scan.) Answer the simple questions. Reread the others carefully, thinking over the entire paragraph if necessary (sometimes going back to the whole picture helps us realize what we need to look for).

Some pointers!

Underline with short lines, or if you're not sure, just mark the region where you think some answers might be with a dot on the margin (First Scanning). You can also write the question number in the margin in the region where you believe the answer is before underlining the answer in the text. This "light highlighting" technique will save you time in the long run. You can also highlight crucial words/points, but not entire sentences, in case it isn't the correct answer, and you get confused afterward!

#5

You should strive to tackle the trickiest aspects and answer those questions in the second scanning (and third, fourth... if you're practicing). Remember that re-reading the easy portions (much faster than the difficult parts) may be required since those ideas may help us understand the harder parts. Take my word for it!

#6

It would help if you were quick. Reread your answers, including the simple ones, to ensure that everything is in order. In our tests, you usually have one minute to copy your answers into the proper answer field.

Remember, you can't be good at something unless you practice it (practice). It is not enough to "understand" or "know" things, and you must be skilled at putting them into action!

Eye exercises for speed reading

Muscles regulate eye movement in your eye sockets and eyeballs, which, like the rest of your muscles, can be strengthened by training. Eye strength is useful for speed reading, which taxes your eyes more than usual reading because it requires your eyes to cover more distance on the page. Making your eye muscles stronger and more flexible improves your visual clarity and slows the natural degradation of your eyesight that occurs with age.

Thumb-to-thumb glancing

Thumb-to-thumb gazing exercises the muscles in your eye sockets that govern peripheral vision and extends the eye muscles in general, making them healthier and more flexible.

To get the most out of this exercise, attempt to look at your thumbs without moving your head.

1. Look straight ahead while sitting or standing, stretch your arms out to your sides, and raise your thumbs.
2. Look back and forth between your left and right thumbs ten times without rotating your head.
3. Steps 1 and 2 must be repeated three times.

Eye writing

This exercise requires you to move your eyes in ways that are unrelated to normal vision, giving them an excellent workout. Eye writing strengthens the extra-ocular muscles of the eye socket and is especially beneficial for strengthening the eyeball's flexibility and range of motion. It doesn't get any easier than this:

1. Take a look at the wall on the other side of the room (or the wall that is farthest away from you).
2. Assume you're writing your name on the wall with your eyes.

In other words, move your gaze as if you were painting your name on the wall with a paintbrush. Try writing your name in block letters first, then in cursive letters.

Hooded eyes

Hooded eyes relax your eyes; repeat this practice two or three times when your eyes need a little break.

1. Close your eyes halfway and focus on keeping your eyelids from trembling. You're relaxing your eyes by concentrating on your eyelids.
2. Look at a distant thing with your eyes partially closed. Your eyes quit trembling.

Squeezing of the eyes

Doing eye squeezes relaxes your eyes, makes your eye muscles more flexible and promotes blood and oxygen flow to your eyes and face. This exercise takes roughly three minutes:

1. As you inhale deeply and slowly, widen your eyes and lips as wide as you can and stretch out all of your facial muscles.
2. Close and compress your eyelids as firmly as you can as you exhale, straining all the muscles in your face, neck, and head and clenching your jaws.
3. Hold your breath and squeeze for 30 seconds.

Steps 1 through 3 should be repeated four times more, followed by a short break and another set of five squeezes.

HOW TO READ FASTER AND RETAIN MORE

Reading is a profound human ability that receives insufficient attention these days. We want everything to be delivered immediately, including information. At this time, most individuals prefer to scroll and surf rather than read. According to a Pew Research Center research, approximately 25% of individuals in America did not read a book at all in 2018.

We don't learn as much when we scroll idly as we do when we read. When avid readers become lost in a book, they experience less anxiety, and reading fosters empathy. There are numerous reasons to read a book on a regular basis; if you want to learn more, see Reading With Purpose Can Change Your Life.

Reading does not have to be a time-consuming activity. If you believe that reading takes too much time, you could attempt fast reading. If you know how to speed read, you can read six times as many books.

When you speed read, you can process much more information than the ordinary individual. According to a recent study, the average adult can read around 300 words per minute, and speed readers can read at a rate of roughly 1,500 words per minute. A fast reader can read five times as many words as the average adult for those keeping score at home. There are a few exceptions that can read even more.

To put that in context, consider that the typical book is roughly 100,000 words long. A book of such length will take the average adult reader about 5.5 hours to read. A fast reader can finish the same activity in around 50 minutes. This offers up tremendous opportunities for fast readers to read a book every day in less than an hour or seven books each week. If they read for an hour per day, the average reader will only appreciate 1.27 novels every week. The average adult will read 66.18 books by the end of the year, whereas the speed reader will read over 365.

Hacks for accelerating your reading

Although speed reading requires some practice, you can begin reaping the benefits of this reading style almost immediately.

The first item you should read is the table of contents

When we begin reading a book, we far too often skip through the table of contents–especially if we want to read the book in its entirety. The table of contents serves as the reader's guide through the book. Because fast readers aren't concerned with memorizing every word, knowing the main points of each chapter prepares their minds to receive the information.

You wouldn't go on a road trip without first reading a map, would you? It makes as much sense to read mindlessly as it does to drive without reading traffic signs. You can read a book without consulting the table of contents, but you're more likely to lose attention or waste time thinking about structural issues that could be answered with a fast glance at the front matter. If you need to know which chapters contain certain information, the table of contents can help you. This allows you to skip over sections that aren't relevant to your inquiry.

The table of contents may not provide much material in some circumstances, or the author may utilize it to urge you to read more. If the table of contents fails to provide indications, a cursory check at the first chapter or two can explain how the author organizes their work.

Always read with a purpose

After you've determined the chapter's topic, keep a question in the back of your mind. Asking yourself, "What is the author attempting to teach me?" is an excellent method to organize your thoughts. As you read, your brain will strive to figure out the answer to this question.

When you read with a goal in mind, you will be able to digest pertinent information while filtering out irrelevant content.

Determine the author's point of view and read just enough references to comprehend

Books typically include references to other scholarly works to support their point of view. You can learn more about how the author will formulate their important arguments by looking at what they chose to cite, and this information can help you think more clearly as you speed read.

When you look at the references, you don't have to stop and read through every note or source. References that just reinforce what the author has said will rapidly become tiresome to read, and you only need to get the gist of it. Continued consumption of the same knowledge will not provide you with any additional benefits after you have enough information to make sense of the material.

Consider reading in the same way that you consider eating. You don't have to eat everything on the buffet just because it's full of good selections. You can move on from the references after you have enough information to understand the notion, just as you would stop eating when you are full.

Never, ever read aloud (or in your head)

Reading aloud helps foster fluency in beginning readers, but it will slow you down. When students read passages aloud at school, it serves a purpose, but it is useless in the context of speed reading.

When we read aloud, our brain has to work a little bit harder than when we read silently. Reading engages the same portions of your brain whether you read the information loudly or silently. The primary distinction between quiet reading and reading aloud is that speaking causes your brain to perform an additional step.

Brocas' Area is the brain area responsible for translating your thoughts into meaningful expression through voice, and Wernicke's Area is in charge of understanding. If you can reduce sub-vocalization while reading aloud, you can avoid reading and comprehending speech in Wernicke's Area before vocalizing it in Broca's Area.

When we read aloud, our brain not only sees the words on the paper, but it also has to go through the effort of hearing the words and creating speech. We don't need to say anything to grasp what we're reading, and the extra steps can drastically slow us down.

You may have observed that you may have difficulty comprehending what you just read when you read aloud, and it may even be required to re-read the same line to ensure that what you observed and spoke are in complete agreement.

When you use the third strategy on this list, reading out loud becomes even more impractical. This strategy necessitates considering material in parts larger than sentences. Working through books paragraph by paragraph to determine the author's point of view is a waste of time; going line by line to develop speech is a waste of time.

It can be challenging to implement all of these tactics at first; therefore, I propose Outread app (https://outreadapp.com/) to assist you to read quicker.

Instead of focusing on every single petal, speed reading is like taking in the scenery of a garden.

When we read at a leisurely speed, we have the opportunity to perceive words in a new light. Consider reading line by line the equivalent of pausing to admire a magnificent flower garden with a magnifying glass or spending thirty minutes viewing a piece of artwork three inches in front of your face. You may believe that you need to look that closely and see some great things, but you are missing the whole picture.

Speed reading allows you to see the big picture, such as how many distinct types of flowers there are or how diverse brush strokes combine to create a unified image. When you look at the big picture, you can make greater sense of what you see.

Instead of wasting time concentrating on the petals of a single flower species, take in the entire garden. Using speed reading comprehension techniques allows you to absorb more of the major concepts from your reading items. You not only learn more from each book you read, but you also get to read new books along the way.

How to improve reading retention

Reading is simple. It only remembers what you read that's difficult. If this is occurring to you, don't feel bad. Many people have difficulty remembering what they have read, and it's quite common. Why? There are numerous causes for this, including a tough subject and simply having too much going on in our lives. However, you do not have to accept it. You can boost your reading retention.

Slow down

You can't read fast enough to remember what you read. The critical word is "slow." The slower you read, the better your brain will recall what you read, and reading slowly allows the brain to digest the information.

Consider it this way: You're traveling down a road you've never been down before at about 25 miles per hour. You have enough time to enjoy the sights and landmarks before returning home. Take the same route at a speed of seventy miles per hour. Do you have the time to capture everything? Are you able to view every street sign?

When you go slowly, you retain more information.

Repeat

Repetition is quite beneficial. I once heard that you'd remember it better if you repeat someone's name three times, which occasionally works for me.

When I instruct my kids to get something when we're out shopping, I make them repeat what I said back to me. That strengthens the conversation for them. They won't go down the incorrect aisle and wonder what they were supposed to acquire. They'll recall saying it to me over and again.

Say the names of the last five vice presidents aloud multiple times to help you recall them. Repeat it over and over, even if you're just reading it from a piece of paper. This information infiltrates your system without your knowledge.

Take notes

Taking notes is another means of repeating what is spoken to oneself. Assume you're sitting in on a politician's speech. You won't remember anything he said, let alone correctly. That is why a journalist takes notes.

Don't copy and paste. Make a list of key points. Please abbreviate in a way that you will understand later. Notes are an excellent tool to reinforce what you hear.

The same is true for reading. If you can, highlight the book as you read. Make notes in a book or a notebook. It's one thing to read it, and making a list of the highlights of what you read will help you recall what you read.

Remove distractions

The television in the background drives me mad when I try to read for school and recall the essential topics, and I have to read passages several times to understand what the author is trying to say. The sound of the children playing is equally loud.

You can't exactly get rid of the kids or the television, no matter how enticing it is. However, you can minimize its impact on you. Turn off the television, and move to a different room. Insert earplugs. Find a study environment that helps you concentrate on what you're reading to remember it.

Review

After you've completed reading, go over the content again. You could do it as soon as you finish reading the information, but you could also do it later. After a few hours or the next day, go over what you've read. Don't read it all over again. Read your notes. Read the headings. Scan it. Review it.

SPEED LISTENING

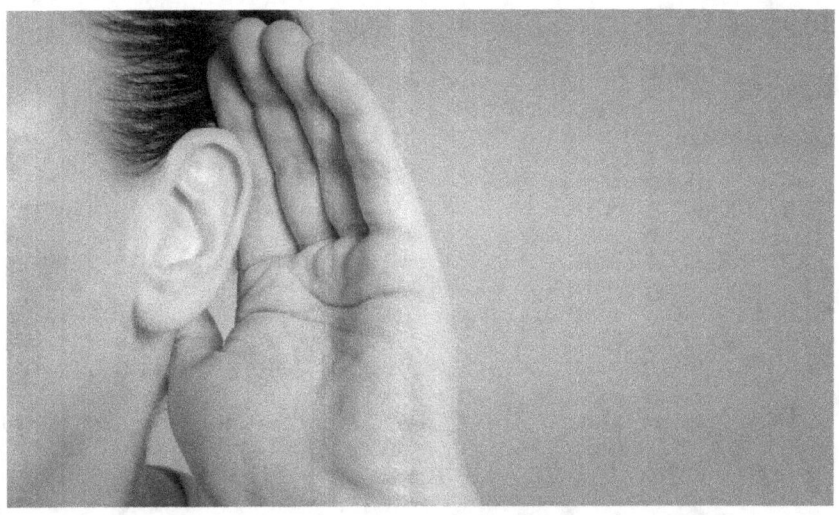

Podcasts, audiobooks, and even YouTube videos can provide valuable information. However, for newcomers, podcasts and audiobooks, in particular, can be time consuming. This is when speed-listening comes into play. Consuming content more quickly has several important advantages.

Increase your content consumption

Listening at double the normal speed, or even 1.5x, permits you to consume more content. You can read or listen to two books in the time it would have taken you to read one. More podcasts can be listened to at the same time. You can eat more of whatever you are speed listening to in the same amount of time.

Even if you don't get every detail, listening to two books quickly is far more helpful than listening to one book slowly. The value you can receive from listening to more books and podcasts rather than listening at standard pace is considerably more, and hence you will benefit.

This may appear obvious, but consider the following example to further understand the benefit. You want to listen to audiobooks, one about productivity to help you be more productive and one that is unique but you know you'll enjoy it. When you listen to things twice as fast as usual, you can read/listen to these books in the time it would have taken you to listen to just one of them. Isn't that fantastic?

The content's quality becomes less important

This may appear unimpressive and undesirable, but consider it from another angle. The more (worthwhile) stuff you can consume, the less important the quality of each individual piece of content becomes. Because you can consume more content, the likelihood that you'll listen to some amazing stuff increases dramatically. So it's not a big concern if you listen to something that doesn't satisfy you.

However, if you only read three novels per year, these must be excellent. If even one of them isn't what you expected and falls short in quality, that means one-third of the written content you ingested was subpar, and you'll wonder if it's even worth looking for new books.

On the other hand, if you read 20 books in a year, not every one of them has to be remarkable. If one of the 19 great books is of poor quality, you won't mind since you'll move on to the next wonderful one.

Reduce the time cost

Obviously, listening to things faster results in them taking less time. Reduced time costs lead to a reduction in the relevance of choice.

When you put the time you've saved into listening to more good information, your chances of discovering something you wouldn't have discovered otherwise skyrocket.

Reducing the time cost of consuming content lowers the barrier to entry for beginning to consume said information. So, if you're having trouble starting to read books and listen to podcasts, rapid listening may be the way to go.

Consider the following example: The Joe Rogan Experience is one of the most well-known podcasts in the world. Joe Rogan, the show's host, interviews a wide range of guests, from Elon Musks to up-and-coming comedians. However, episodes are often 90 to 120 minutes long. That's a lot of time, and even if the information is mainly great, two hours can be a lot. So, if you listen to the two-hour podcast at twice the speed, which is doable after approximately a week of speed listening, the entire episode will take up only one hour. What you do with the remaining hour is entirely up to you; will you watch other stuff or meditate? You make the call.

Drawbacks

Naturally, listening to things at twice the pace has its drawbacks. One of them is that you might overlook something. While this is undeniably true, the things you miss when you don't read as much are far more significant. Again, it boils down to the utilitarian viewpoint that listening to multiple things at double the pace is more valuable than listening to just one thing at the ordinary rate.

Another disadvantage that is frequently mentioned in the context of fast listening is the belief that you do not enjoy what you are listening to or viewing as much as you would otherwise. This is not the situation in my instance. Rereading Harry Potter at 2x speed is equally as enjoyable as reading it at normal pace. Slowing down the climactic speed, in particular, improves the overall plot. You must also distinguish why you watch or listen to stuff. If I'm procrastinating and want to kill time on YouTube, I don't want to consume more content in the same amount of time because I've already scheduled time to view some videos. However, if I want to read a book that a friend recommended because it has wonderful information, I want to get it as soon as possible, therefore I listen to the Audiobook at 2x speed.

Getting started

Starting to speed up and listen to content might be challenging because our brains must adjust to the increased speed. However, our minds are quite quick to pick up on new information, and it won't be long before you're listening to things at twice the speed.

To begin, select a speed that is still understandable to you but not completely comfortable listening to. After a few minutes, your brain will have acclimated to the new speed, and you will be able to increase the playback speed even further.

Pushing yourself to listen faster has no end. However, I've discovered that breaching the 2.5x barrier is difficult, therefore I keep to 2 or 2.5x listening speed.

Even though it seemed strange and weird at first, it didn't take me long to get to 2x speed, approximately two weeks.

CONCLUSION

The capacity to learn new things rapidly is a huge benefit. People who can quickly comprehend new concepts, learn and use new and effective skills, and absorb new information have a considerable advantage over those who struggle to learn.

Is speed learning restricted for a small group of people endowed with a rare intellectual gift? Is it exclusively for the "geniuses" among us?

"No," is the answer.

Every one of us can learn to learn faster, and a few basic tools can assist us. Suppose we commit to mastering these techniques via habit. In that case, we will see enormous improvements in our ability to acquire concepts quickly, process new information in less time, and rapidly grow our abilities and knowledge.

Unfortunately, the majority of people do not take advantage of this opportunity. This is because skills like reading are not something that arose or existed in nature. Reading is an ability that humans developed, and since humans developed it, it is not an instinctual skill that we are born with, and it's a talent that needs to be mastered.

Most of us learn to read, but not all of us learn to read effectively and comprehend. Our educational systems, instructors, and parents do an excellent job of teaching us how to put words together to form sentences. However, they don't always show us how to use our powerful eyes and minds most beneficially. This could not be more untrue. We just need to learn how to use our infinitely strong eyes and minds in the right way.

This book does not involve learning or doing something new or complicated since the eyes and mind already can interpret knowledge at a high level.

What it takes is just a few minor changes in reading habits.

www.ingramcontent.com/pod-product-compliance
Lightning Source LLC
Chambersburg PA
CBHW070053120526
44588CB00033B/1416